The New Psychology

Its Message, Principles and Practice

by

William Walker Atkinson

Contents

Chapter I.	The New Psychology.
Chapter II.	The Ego, or Self.
Chapter III.	Egoism, Not Egotism.
Chapter IV.	Consciousness and Beyond.
Chapter V.	The Subconscious.
Chapter VI.	The Superconscious.
Chapter VII.	Impressions.
Chapter VIII.	Perception.
Chapter IX.	Mental Paths.
Chapter X.	Thought And Character.
Chapter XI.	Emotion.
Chapter XII.	Imagination.
Chapter XIII.	Memory.
Chapter XIV.	Desire.
Chapter XV.	The Will.
Chapter XVI.	Thinking: Conscious and Subconscious.
Chapter XVII.	Mental Suggestion.
Chapter XVIII.	Auto-Suggestion.
Chapter XIX.	Mind and Body.
Chapter XX.	Positive and Negative Qualities.

Chapter I.

The New Psychology.

Psychology is the science of the mind. Its field is the scientific study of the mind; its functions; its laws; its activities. The study of psychology embraces the consideration of the various mental states, both in the conscious and subconscious fields, including "sensations, desires, emotions, cognitions, reasonings, decisions, volitions, and the like," as Prof. Wm. James has so well stated it.

Psychology is no new science. Its history extends far back in the story of the intellectual evolution of the race. For a time it was considered but a branch of the general subject of metaphysics, and partook of the general fogginess of that branch of thought. But gradually emerging from the fog it stood at last clearly defined as a scientific study rather than as a branch of metaphysics or philosophy. Like any other science, it is based upon ascertained facts and laws, rather than upon assumed abstract theories. Leaving behind it the conflicting theories regarding the ultimate nature of the mind, it concerns itself solely with the actual workings, activities, and operations of the mind, and the laws that appear to govern these. Instead of evolving theories of the origin and ultimate nature of the mind and then working from the theory down to facts to fit in

The New Psychology

with the theory, psychology began to pursue scientific methods and proceeded to examine facts and phenomena in order to work back to fundamental principles. Leaving to metaphysics and philosophy the speculations regarding abstract mind and its relation to the soul, psychology devoted its entire attention to a careful and scientific examination of the working laws of the mind, their effects, consequences, conditions, and general mode of operation.

But even when this stage had heen gained, psychology failed to take its practical place in the affairs of the every-day life of the people. Although divorced from the vague speculations of metaphysics and philosophy, and confining itself to provable facts and principles, psychology still retained more or less of an abstract and non-practical aspect to the majority of the race. Although considering facts and principles in a scientific manner, and adhering to the "how" rather than to the "why" features of mental activities, psychology still failed to take its place in the list of the sciences that were capable of *actual application* in the lives of the people. While recognized as a necessary part of the mental equipment of the educated man or woman, yet it was regarded by the masses as something impractical and not useful. The question "What is it good for?" was pertinently asked by practical people of affairs. "How can I use it?" "What will it do for me?" "Of what benefit is it?"—these questions were asked concerning it by the general public. And the answer was not furnished.

But arising from this demand, actual or implied, there arose a new set of psychologists who unwittingly laid the foundations of that which is now called "The New Psychology." These pioneers began working along the lines of a utilitarian psychology—a psychology that could be *used* in every-day life, a psychology that was workable. These pioneers did not use the term "The New Psychology;" nor did they realize that they were leading the science from the abstract place it had hitherto occupied. They merely sought to put into application the principles already discovered—to enable people to "do things" with these principles, rather than to merely contemplate them as something a little different from metaphysical and philosophical principles, but yet very similar in nature. These men and women were the unconscious workers along the lines of what is now called the pragmatic school of thought—the school that holds that the truth and value of a science, philosophy, or idea, consists of its value when applied and set to work—"What will it do?" "How will it work out?" "What can be done with it?" "What is it good for?" being the tests applied by this new school of thought.

And upon the foundations erected by these earlier practical thinkers has arisen the edifice of "The New Psychology," or rather the first stories of that edifice, for the building is still going on and the structure seems destined to far exceed in grandeur and magnificence even the fondest dreams of its earlier workers. The New Psychology has made wonderful strides since the beginning of the present century. Although its foundations were laid in the preceding century, still the actual "above the ground" work has been done during the last eight years, and it may be justly considered as a product of the Twentieth Century. Some of the old-school thinkers protest against this application of the pragmatic test to psychology, claiming that it should be allowed to remain in the realm of abstract thought. But these people are pulling against the tide of evolution, and are practically setting their faces against the entire trend of modern thought and activity. The tendency of the age is decidedly utilitarian, and the pragmatic test is being rigidly applied to everything in the realm of thought. "What is it good for?" "What can we do with it!" "How will it help us!" these are the characteristic questions of the age, and all that is offered to the public mind must be subjected to that test, and must live or die according to its degree of success in meeting the requirements.

The New Psychology

The New Psychology is practical, workable, and usable, first, last and all the time. Its very existence depends upon its agreement with these principles. The entire effort of its workers and teachers is in the direction of rendering practicable the laws of the mind. It is no longer a matter of informing people "just what" are certain mental faculties or states; nor even "just how" they operate. The new psychologist hastens to inform his students just what these principles and laws mean to him in the direction of increasing his mental efficiency, strengthening his positive qualities, and restraining and inhibiting his negative faculties and qualities. The student is informed of the various mental qualities he possesses, and the laws of their operation, but (and herein lies the difference between the old and the new psychology) he is also taught how these laws may be applied to the strengthening, improving, and upbuilding of his mental being. Character-building, in the new psychology, has been taken from its old position of a subject for lectures, sermons, and admonitions along the lines of good advice and wise counsel, and has been placed well to the front as a practical field for experiment, practice, and actual accomplishment. The student is no longer forced to content himself with the statement "You should do so-and-so"—he is now taught just how this "so-and-so" may be done. He is taught the practical work of "making himself over" according to well tested, and plainly stated methods and principles.

Another important feature of the work of the new psychology has been the raising of certain little-understood phases of mental activity from the region of the occult and mystical, and the placing of them among the recognized and at least partially understood phenomena of psychology. Much that was formerly regarded as a part of "abnormal psychology" is now freely accorded a place in the normal psychology of the schools. We refer especially to that wonderful field of mental activity outside of the range of consciousness, generally known as the "sub-conscious," "subjective" or "subliminal" fields.

The New Psychology

Formerly regarded as belonging to the abnormal phases of mental action, these fields are now regarded as containing within them at least nine-tenths of our mental activities. The field of consciousness is now recognized as comprising but a very small portion of the activities of the mind. And accordingly The New Psychology has devoted considerable of its activities to the exploration of those hitherto unsuspected regions of the mind, and the result has been that many strange and wonderful things have been discovered, scientifically examined, and classified. And in this exploration, the investigators have succeeded in throwing much light upon many dark subjects that had previously either been denied or else attributed to the supernatural. The New Psychology has succeeded in showing that, so far as its investigations have extended, there is no super-natural—that everything is natural—that what has been considered super-natural is merely natural phenomena the nature of which has not been understood—that natural law and order is ever in evidence in these newly understood phases of the mind.

And, true to its pragmatic origin, The New Psychology has not contented itself with a mere exploration and examination of these sub-conscious regions of the mind. It no sooner discovers, examines and classifies than it begins to consider the "workable" and "usable" features of the thing. It begins to consider and plan just how these may be turned to account in the every-day lives of the people, both in the region of developing desirable qualities and in the restraining and inhibiting of the undesirable ones. The "what is it" is followed by the "how does it act," and then speedily is heard the "how can it be used—the what is it good for" of the pragmatist.

And this is the spirit in which this book upon The New Psychology is written. Very little time and space is devoted to theory or speculation regarding the "why." The object and intent of the work is closely bound up in the "how" phase of the subject, particularly the "how" of its usability and workability.

THE NEW PSYCHOLOGY

The pragmatic idea is adhered to throughout the entire work, with the ever present consciousness of the "what is it good for"—"what can I do with it." Steering close to the point of "how to do things," we trust that we shall be able to carry our student-passengers safely over the seas of The New Psychology to the haven of Successful Accomplishment.

Chapter II.

The Ego, or Self.

THE OLD treatises on psychology generally began with a consideration of the nature of mind. Some authorities held to the metaphysical conception of the immaterial nature of mind; while others held that mind was a product or manifestation of the brain, and therefore was material in nature. But The New Psychology has preferred to leave this discussion in the hands of the teachers of other branches of philosophy and science, particularly as the old psychologists almost invariably concluded the discussion by the admission that mind in its ultimate nature was unknowable. The later writers have agreed with the writer who said that "Psychology is no more bound to begin by telling what mind is, than physics is obliged to start by settling the vexed question as to what matter is." And as physics is concerned only with the phenomena of matter, so is the new conception of psychology concerned only with the phenomena of mind.

We have thought that the logical requirements of the case indicated that we should begin our consideration of the general subject of The New Psychology by an examination of the subject of the Ego, or Self, which we find at the center of all conscious mental action, and, in a way, at the center of all unconscious mental action. To consider the ego, or self, from a purely scientific and psychological viewpoint is a somewhat difficult undertaking, particularly as the special subject is generally considered to belong to the field of metaphysics or philosophy into which field we have announced our intention to avoid trespassing. But we think that there is a way of regarding the ego, or self, from a strictly psychological position and viewpoint, and to this consideration we now invite you.

All intelligent persons make use of the mental concept of "I"—of that individual consciousness which is the thinker of the thought, the feeler of the feeling, the actor of the act, the willer of the deed. All attempts to define or explain the nature of this "I" must fail—it is a something that cannot be explained, and is known only by its own presence in consciousness. At the last, our consciousness reports that it is—without informing us why, how, or what it is. Think as we will, we are inevitably brought back to this position, just where we started—the "I" *is*—and nothing more. To every conscious individual there is always a perception of the "I" in the consciousness of "I am." In every thought, feeling, and manifestation of will there is always this consciousness of "I am" in the individual. It is always "I" think; or "I" feel; or "I" will—always the "I" behind the mental state, and to which every feeling is referred; which participates in every thought; and from which emanates every effort of the will. Every reference to a mental state within us brings us to a realization of the presence of this "I." With every individual it is always "I am." The individual can never truthfully say "I am not." This "I" which *is*, is the knower, the actor, the thinker, the seer, the doer. It is the essence of each and every mental state.

To many persons the perception of the "I," or ego, or self, is very clear and distinct. But to others it is more or less involved in the consciousness of the secondary "I"; subordinate self; alter-ego; or the "Me," as Prof. Wm. James calls it. Perhaps the best way to enable the student to distinguish the "Me" from the" I" will be to consider the latter at first, and then to lead him

The Ego, or Self

to consider and recognize the true ego or "I." The distinction is somewhat subtle, but a little consideration will reveal it to you. The essential difference is that the "I" is the *Something* that knows, feels, and wills, while the "Me" is that part of the self that is known to the "I" as mental states, feelings, thoughts, and will-impulses. A man's body, and physical sensations, etc., are a part of his "Me" which may be examined, considered, and ruled by his "I." His feelings, pains, pleasures, prejudices, opinions, inclinations and the rest of the mental things that he considers to be part of himself, are all portions of the "Me," for all of them may be examined, changed, and ruled by the "I." The "Me" in all its parts and phases is always the "object" of contemplation by the "I"—that is, *that toward which* the powers of the "I" are extended. And the "I" is always the "subject" of its contemplation of the things of the "Me"—that is, *that which is the essence* of the contemplation. Let us consider a few examples, in order to understand this a little more clearly.

You see a thing. There are three phases of the seeing—namely: (1) the thing seen, which is something outside of both the "I" and the "Me;" (2) the mental operation known as "sight" which belongs to the "Me;" and (3) the Something that *sees*, which is the "I." This same rule applies to all of the five senses. This is the simplest example—we have others, more complex and subtle, before us. We experience the "feeling" arising from some emotional activity. There are three phases of this feeling—namely: (1) the outside thing from which the emotion arises; (2) the emotion felt, which belongs to the "Me," for it comes from within our being; and (3) the feeler of the emotion or feeling—that *Something* that experiences it, which is the "I." We think a thought. There are three phases to this also—to-wit: (1) the outer object of the thought; (2) the thought itself, which belongs to the "Me;" (3) the Thinker, which is the "I."

Leaving out of consideration the outside thing which causes the sense-impression, the emotional feeling, or the thought, we have two aspects of mental activity to deal with—(1) the mental activity itself; and (2) the "I" which is always the Knower of the mental activity. The mental activity is the object, and the "I" is the subject of consciousness. These two elements are always present in thought and feeling—in all conscious mental activity. They are opposites—the two ends of the mental stick. We may carefully examine a thought or feeling, and see it in all of its aspects—but who or what is it that examines and sees it? The "I." We may decide to accept or reject certain ideas, feelings, or thoughts, and we recognize the power in ourselves to do this to a greater or lesser degree. But what is this *Something* which feels that it can change or govern the idea, thought or feeling—which knows that it may choose to do this or that; to will to do or not to do? The "I." This idea is the Self—the Master. We cannot escape from it—it is the essence of all that is individual in us. This "I" is what psychologists have called the "pure ego." It is the *Something* that is always present in consciousness as *that which is conscious*, while the "Me" is simply a bundle of states of consciousness, or things of which the "I" is conscious. The "I" is the Thinker; the Knower; the Feeler; the Actor. The "Me" is constantly changing—the "Me" of to-day is different from the "Me" of yesterday, and the latter different from the "Me" of the day before. And yet the "I" is always the same—always the "I," for other than itself it cannot be.

Just what is this "I" we cannot tell. This riddle has never been solved by the mind of man. So subtle is the essence of the "I" that it is almost impossible to think of it as a *something* apart from the mental states of the "Me." All that can be said of it is that it is. Its only report of itself is "I am." Is what? I am *what?* You cannot answer these questions unless you bring in the attributes and qualities of the "Me," for in one sense the "I" is *nothing* without these qualities. And yet, every advanced thinker has learned to recognize the "I am" report of the Self, as distinct from the qualities of the "Me." You cannot examine the "I" by the "I." You must have an object for your subject, and if you make the "I" your object, then you have no subject to examine

The Ego, or Self

it. You place the "I" under the mental microscope to examine it, and lo! you have nothing to look through the glass—the "I" is at the wrong end of the glass. You cannot even consider the "I" in imagination. You may imagine your body, or your mental states, thoughts, feelings, sense impressions, ideas, or actions—these belong to the 'Me" and are objective in nature. But the moment you begin to try to imagine the "I," you find that you cannot get outside of yourself in order to examine yourself. You cannot be at both ends of the glass at the same time. You cannot be both bat and ball at the same time. Try as you may you will find that you cannot stand aside and examine the "I," as you have found you can do with the "Me." You have found a final, ultimate *Something* within yourself that defies your powers of analysis, or examination. You demand of yourself the answer of your inner nature, and your answer to yourself is simply "I am." Further than this you cannot say, without going outside of yourself into the "Me."

There are several things, however, that you may learn about the "I" by a negative process of exclusion. You may find that you are not able to think of your "I" as not-being. You can never say "I am not," nor can you even *imagine* yourself as not-being. So long as you think of yourself—the "I"—at all, you must accompany the thought with the consciousness of being. You cannot even imagine yourself out of existence. That is, while you may imagine another "I" as not-being; or even imagine your own "I" as fading into nothingness, in an abstract way; a little analysis will show you that in the latter instance you are not thinking of your "I" at all, but of an abstract "something" not yourself at all, for while you are thinking this abstract something out of existence you will find a consciousness of the "I" seeing that "something else" fading away—it cannot so think of *itself*. Nor can you imagine yourself as being any other "I" than what it is. You may think of it surrounded with other "Me" aspects or objects—personalities, and environments. But you can never think of your "I" as being another "I." The consciousness of the "I" is above personality—it is something inseparable from individuality.

We might pursue this consideration much further, but we are approaching too nearly the thin dividing line between psychology and metaphysics. The consciousness of the "I" is an actual experience, just as much as is the consciousness of the page before you, and therefore is a fit subject for psychological notice. We have called your attention to it in a somewhat unusual way, for we hold that the whole subject of The New Psychology is bound up with this recognition of the "I"—that it revolves around this "I" as a wheel around its center. We regard all of the mental faculties, powers, organs, qualities, and modes of expression, as merely instruments, tools, or channels of expression of this wonderful Something—the Self, the pure Ego—the "I."

And this is the message of The New Psychology—that You, the "I," have at your command a wonderful array of mental instruments, tools, machinery, which if properly used may create for yourself any kind of personality you may desire. You are the Master Workman who may make of yourself what you will. But before you can appreciate this truth—before you can make it your own—before you can apply it—you must enter into a recognition and realization of this wonderful "I" that you are, to which body, and senses, yea, even the mind itself, are but channels of expression. You are something more than body, or senses, or mind—you are that wonderful Something, master of all these things, but of which you can say but one thing: "I am."

Chapter III.

Egoism, Not Egotism.

To some, it might appear that the suggestions concerning the recognition of the Ego advanced in the preceding chapter are calculated to encourage the quality of egotism among those accepting the advice. As a matter of fact the true recognition of the pure Ego is diametrically opposed to the objectionable trait or quality generally known as "egotism." In egotism we find the person filled with an overweening sense of the importance and qualities of his personality. He imagines that he is not as other men, and that he is immensely superior to them, and of far greater relative importance. The egotist is wrapped up in his personality, and the things of the "Me." It is always "me and mine" with him. And unfortunately there has been a great confusion in the meaning of the term "egoism," by reason of the objectionable characteristics of "egotism." The two terms have been regarded as identical, although they are as far apart as the poles.

It is only when we pass by the common acceptation of the term "egoism," and consider it in its philosophical aspect, that we may begin to understand its real meaning. In the first place it is not connected with the attributes of *personality*—it concerns itself solely with *individuality*. The egoist does not compare his personality with that of others, for he regards personality as a something belonging to him and yet not himself. His sense of the Ego consists in the recognition of the reality of the "I" which is his real self, and consequently the things of personality fade into comparative insignificance. As an old writer has said: "Whether we try to avoid it or not, we must face this reality sometime—the reality of our own Egohood—that which makes us say "I," and in saying "I" leads to the discovery of a new world." As to the confusion regarding egoism and egotism, the same writer has said: "Our Ego tells us of the duties we owe others, because they are 'I's' as we are." And another old writer informs us of the ideal individual, of whom he says: "With that union of intellectual Egoism and moral unselfishness which is a characteristic of his large and liberal nature." So you see that egoism is a far different thing from the quality known as egotism.

Egoism, as the term is used in this book, is the doctrine of the reality of the Ego or "I," and of its recognition and realization. It is the recognition, realization, and manifestation of the "I" of the individual. It teaches that man is not merely the composite of his feelings, emotions, and ideas, but that he is a *Something* back of and under these mental states and activities—something that is, or should be, the Master of these secondary things. It is not necessary to accept any particular theory or idea regarding the nature of the "I" in order to manifest its powers. Whether the "I" be the "soul," or whether it be a center of conscious energy in a world-soul, or whether it be simply a focus of the universal energy of material science, it matters not; the important thing about it in psychology is that it is, and may be recognized, realized, and manifested. And in this recognition, realization, and manifestation is to be found the keynote of The New Psychology.

It may be objected to, that it can make no material difference to the individual whether he is able to distinguish between the "I" and the "Me" or not—that he must live his life according to his nature in either case. But this contention is not correct, for the realization of the "I" at once causes the individual to know that "he" is not merely what he thinks, feels and wills, but is rather a *Something* that thinks, feels, and wills, and may govern and master these mental activities, instead of being governed and mastered by them. There is a vast difference in this point of view. There is the greatest difference from the pragmatic point of view, for according to the old idea the man is a slave and a creature of his mental states, while under the new idea he may assume his rightful place on the mental throne, and make his choice as to what feelings he may wish to feel; what emotions he may wish to experience; what thoughts he may wish to think; what things he may wish to do. In short, the Egoist becomes the Master, instead of the slave. He realizes that the sovereign will of the individual resides in the Ego, and that even his mental states must obey its mandates.

The average man is a slave to his thoughts, ideas, and feelings. He is governed by inherited tendencies, and the suggestions of other minds. He allows his feelings to run away with him, and does not realize that he may regulate and govern them, changing and inhibiting them at will. He thinks that he is *what he seems to be*, and fails to understand that he may make himself that which *he wishes to be*. The average person is a mere puppet of environment and outside influences. He is moved along like an automaton. He is simply his "Me," and does not realize that he is an "I." He is swept from his feet by waves of feeling that he is utterly unable to repress or control, and is a creature of his own feelings and moods. He does not realize what Self-Mastery is—the words convey no meaning to him, for he does not recognize the Self. He is mastered by the "Me," instead of mastering by the "I." The men who have risen from the ranks, and who stand head and shoulders above their fellows in mental achievement have invariably realized the "I," although they may never have reasoned it out consciously—their recognition may have been intuitive. But all men and women who have "done things" have found this "I" within and beyond the "Me."

This mastery by the "I" opens up an entirely new world of thought, feeling, and activity to the individual. To be able to make of oneself what one will is truly a wonderful thing. To think what one wants to think, feel what one wants to feel, do what one wants to do—surely this is an achievement worthy of a Master. And it is possible to those who will take the time and trouble to acquire the art of Self-Mastery and Self-Expression.

We shall not dwell upon this idea at length at this point, for the idea will permeate the entire work, and will be brought out in reference to every phase of mentation. But, before passing on to the next chapter, we would like you to consider the following words of Edward Carpenter in reference to the state of the ordinary man who is ruled by his mind, instead of ruling it. Carpenter says: "We moderns…are unaccustomed to the mastery over our own inner thoughts and feelings. That a man should be a prey to any thought that chances to take possession of his mind, is commonly among us assumed as unavoidable. It may be a matter of regret that he should be kept awake all night from anxiety as to the issue of a lawsuit on the morrow, but that he should have the power of determining whether he be kept awake or not seems an extravagant demand. The image of an impending calamity is no doubt odious, but its very odiousness (we say) makes it haunt the mind all the more pertinaciously, and it is useless to try to expel it. Yet this is an absurd position—for man, the heir of all the ages, to be in: Hag-ridden by the flimsy creatures of his own brain. If a pebble in our boot torments us, we expel it. We take off the boot and shake it out. And once the matter is fairly understood, it is just as easy to expel an intruding and obnoxious thought from the mind. About this there ought to be no mistake, no two opinions. The thing is obvious, clear and unmistakable. It should be as easy to expel an obnoxious thought from the mind as to shake a stone out of your shoe; and till a man can do that, it is just nonsense to talk about his ascendency over Nature, and all the rest of it. He is a mere slave, and a prey to the bat-winged phantoms that flit through the corridors of his own brain. Yet the weary and careworn faces that we meet by thousands, even among the affluent classes of civilization, testify only too clearly how seldom this mastery is obtained. How rare indeed to meet a *man!* How common rather to discover a creature hounded on by tyrant thoughts (or cares, or desires), cowering, wincing under the lash—or perchance priding himself to run merrily in obedience to a driver that rattles the reins and persuades him that he is free—whom he cannot converse with in careless *tete-a-tete* because that alien presence is always there, on the watch."

The same authority continues: "It is one of the prominent doctrines...that the power of expelling thoughts, or, if need be, killing them dead on the spot, *must* be attained. Naturally the art requires practice, but like other arts, when once acquired there is no mystery or difficulty about it. And it is worth practice. It may indeed fairly be said that life only begins when this art has been acquired. For obviously when, instead of being ruled by individual thoughts, the whole flock of them in their immense multitude and variety and capacity is ours to direct and despatch and employ where we list, life becomes a thing so vast and grand, compared with what it was before, that its former condition may well appear almost ante-natal. If you can kill a thought dead, for the time being, you can do anything else with it that you please. And therefore it is that this power is so valuable. And it not only frees a man from mental torment (which is nine-tenths at least of the torment of life), but it gives him a concentrated power of handling mental work absolutely unknown to him before. The two things are co-relative to each other. While at work your thought is to be absolutely concentrated in it, undistracted by anything whatever irrelevant to the matter in hand—pounding away like a great engine, with giant power and perfect economy—no wear and tear of friction, or dislocation of parts owing to the working of different forces at the same time. Then when the work is finished, if there is no more occasion for the use of the machine, it must stop equally, absolutely—stop entirely—no *worrying* (as if a parcel of boys were allowed to play their devilments with a locomotive as soon as it was in the shed)—and the man must retire into that region of his consciousness where his true self dwells. I say that the power of the thought-machine itself is enormously increased by this faculty of letting it alone on the one hand, and of using it singly and with concentration on the other. It becomes a true tool, which a master-workman lays down when done with, but which only a bungler carries about with him all the time to show that he is the possessor of it. Then on and beyond the work turned out by the tool itself is the knowledge that comes to us apart from its use; when the noise of the workshop is over, and mallet and plane laid aside—the faint sounds coming through the open window from the valley and the far seashore; the dim fringe of diviner knowledge which begins to grow, poor thing, as soon as the eternal click-clack of thought is over—the extraordinary intuitions, perceptions, which, though partaking in some degree of the character of the thought, spring from entirely different conditions, and are the forerunners of a changed consciousness."

The same writer then considers the subject of desires, as mastered by the Ego, as follows: "As already said, the subjection of Thought is closely related to the subjection of Desire, and has consequently its specially moral as well as its specially intellectual relation to the question in hand. Nine-tenths of the scattered or sporadic thought with which the mind usually occupies itself when not concentrated on any definite work, is what may be called self-thought—thought of a kind which dwells on and exaggerates the sense of self. This is hardly realized in its full degree till the effort is made to suppress it; and one of the most excellent results of such an effort is that with the stilling of all the phantoms which hover around the lower self, one's

Egoism, Not Egotism

relations to others, to one's friends, to the world at large, and one's perception of all that is concerned in these relations come out into a purity and distinctness unknown before. Obviously, when the mind is full of little desires and fears which concern the local self, and is clouded over by the thought-images which such desires and fears evoke, it is impossible that it should see and understand the greater facts beyond and its own relation to them. But with the subsiding of the former, the great Vision begins to dawn; and a man never feels less alone than when he has ceased to think whether he is alone or not."

In this somewhat extended quotation from Mr. Carpenter, will be seen clearly the idea of Egoism as opposed to Egotism—the mastering of the personality by the individuality, rather than the undue importance attaching to mere personality which is the basis of egotism. Mr. Carpenter's remarks, while uttered in connection with an entirely different subject, nevertheless convey a vital message in connection with The New Psychology, and accordingly we have reprinted them in this work feeling that he has stated the matter in a most forcible and clear manner, in words likely to be remembered by those who read them.

Chapter IV.

Consciousness and Beyond.

It comes as a surprise to the average person to be informed that at least ninety-five per cent of his mental activities are performed on planes of his mind below and above the field of consciousness. The average person is in the habit of thinking of his mind as being limited entirely to the conscious field, whereas that conscious field is but little more than the field of vision of the microscope as compared with the space beyond it from which emerge and disappear the organisms in the drop of water placed in the object-slide—or the field of vision of the telescope as compared with the expanse of the heavens toward which the tube is pointed. Just as there are degrees of heat and cold beyond the field of our instruments—light vibrations below and above the visible spectrum—sounds below and above our capacity for registering them—so are there mental operations constantly being performed out of the narrow; field of consciousness which we have been fondly considering as "our mind."

In perhaps no other branch has The New Psychology made such rapid strides as in this bringing into recognition of the vast area of the mind of man beyond the conscious field. When we consider the accepted ideas on the subject entertained by the students of psychology of to-day, as compared with the ideas of only a few decades back, we may begin to realize the great strides in this branch of thought. Leibnitz was the first great thinker among the Western people to call attention to the fact of the extent and importance of the out-of-conscious mental planes, although the Hindu philosophies are full of references to it. And after Leibnitz's time the progress of the idea was very slow, and it is only within the last twenty years that the text-books on psychology have given to the subject the attention it merited. To-day it is fully recognized by the best authorities.

The following quotations from some of the best authorities may surprise some of you who are not familiar with the idea. Lewes says: "The teaching of most modern psychologists is that *consciousness forms but a small item in the total of psychical processes.* Unconscious sensations, ideas, and judgments are made to play a great part in their explanations. It is very certain that in every conscious volition—every act that is so characterized—the larger part of it is quite unconscious. It is equally certain that in every perception there are unconscious processes of reproduction and inference—there is a middle distance of subconsciousness, and a background of unconsciousness." Hamilton says: "The sphere of our consciousness is only a small circle in a center of a far wider sphere of action and passion, of which we are only conscious through its effects." Taine says: "Mental events imperceptible to consciousness are far more numerous than the others, and of the world which makes up our being we only perceive the highest points—the lighted-up peaks of a continent whose lower levels remain in the shade. Beneath ordinary sensations are their components, that is to say, the elementary sensations, which must be combined into groups to reach our consciousness. Outside a little luminous circle lies a large ring of twilight, and beyond this an indefinite night; but the events of this twilight and this night are as real as those within the luminous circle."

Consciousness and Beyond

Maudsley says: "Examine closely and without bias the ordinary mental operations of daily life, and you will surely discover that consciousness has not one-tenth part of the function therein which it is commonly assumed to have. In every conscious state there are at work conscious, subconscious, and infraconscious energies, the last as indispensable as the first."

Kay says: "Formerly consciousness was regarded as being co-extensive with mind—the mind being held to be conscious of all its own activities, of all the changes or modifications that take place in it. Leibnitz was the first to confute this opinion, and to establish the doctrine that there are energies always at work, and modifications constantly taking place in the mind, of which we are quite unconscious. Since his time this opinion has been gradually gaining ground, and now it is a generally received doctrine in philosophy." Carpenter says: "The psychologists of Germany have taught that much of our mental work is done without consciousness." Hamilton says of the idea that: "The fact of such latent modifications is now established beyond a rational doubt; and on the supposition of their reality we are able to solve various psychological phenomena otherwise inexplicable." Halleck says: "It must not be supposed that the mind is at any one time conscious of all its materials and powers. At any moment we are not conscious of a thousandth part of what we know. It is well that such is the case; for when we are studying an object under a microscope, trying to memorize poetry, demonstrating a geometrical proposition, or learning a Latin verb, we should not want all we knew of history or physics, or images of the persons, trees, dogs, birds, or horses, that we remembered, to rush into our minds at the same time. If they did so our mental confusion would be indescribable. Between the perception and the recall, the treasures of memory, are metaphorically speaking, away from the eye of consciousness. How these facts are preserved, before they are reproduced by the call of memory, consciousness can never tell us. An event may not be thought of for fifty years, and then it may suddenly appear in consciousness. As we grow older the subconscious field increases. When we first began to walk, we were conscious of every step. Later, we can talk about the deepest subjects while we are walking, and not even think of the steps we are taking. We sometimes wind our watches without being conscious of the operation, as is shown by the fact that we again test them to see if we have wound them."

Prof. Gates has said: "At least ninety per cent of our mental life is subconscious. If you will analyze your mental operations you will find that conscious thinking is never a continuous line of consciousness, but a series of conscious data with great intervals of subconsciousness. We sit and try to solve a problem and fail. Suddenly an idea dawns that leads to a solution of the problem. The subconscious processes were at work. We do not volitionally create our own thinking. It takes place in us. We are more or less passive recipients. We cannot change the nature of a thought, but we can, as it were, guide the ship by a moving of the helm." Schofield says: "Our conscious mind, as compared with the unconscious mind, has been likened to the visible spectrum of the sun's rays, as compared to the invisible part which stretches indefinitely on either side. We know now that the chief part of heat comes from the ultra-red rays that show no light; and the main part of the chemical changes in the vegetable world are the results of the other end of the spectrum, which are equally invisible to the eye, and are recognized only by their potent effects. Indeed as these invisible rays extend indefinitely on both sides of the visible spectrum, so we may say that the mind includes not only the visible or conscious part, and what we have called the subconscious, but also the supraconscious mind that lies at the other end—all those regions of higher soul and spirit life, of which we are only at times vaguely conscious, but which always exist, and link us on to veritable verities, on the one side, as surely as the subconscious mind links us with the body on the other."

Consciousness and Beyond

Sir Oliver Lodge has written the remarkable statement regarding the "out-of-conscious" states or planes of the mind: "Let us imagine, then, as a working hypothesis, that our subliminal self—the other and greater part of us—is in touch with another order of existence, and that it is occasionally able to communicate, or somehow, perhaps unconsciously, transmit to the fragment in the body something of the information accessible to it. This guess, if permissible, would contain a clew to a possible explanation of clairvoyance. We should then be like icebergs floating in an ocean, with only a fraction exposed to sun and air and observation: the rest—by far the greater bulk, eleven-twelfths—submerged in a connecting medium, submerged and occasionally in subliminal or sub-aqueous contact with others, while still the peaks, the visible bergs, are far separate. One cannot but sympathize to some extent with those philosophers who urge that the progress of humanity has been achieved by attention to a development of our full-consciousness, and that reversion to the subconscious or to-dream states is a step back. It must be noted, however, that the adjective 'subliminal,' as we understand it, is not suggestive of subordinate or subsidiary, but is far more nearly related to 'sublime;' a statement which, considered objectively, the philosophers in question would probably disallow. If they mean that for the active and practical concerns of life consciousness must be our guide and our adviser, I am with them; but if they mean (as I am sure they do not, when pressed) that inspiration is attained through consciousness, or that it is unlawful and unfruitful to investigate the subconscious, where (I suggest) lie the roots of the connection between mind and matter, then I must join issue with them. So might an iceberg, glorying in its crisp solidity and sparkling pinnacles, resent attention paid to its submerged subliminal supporting region, or to the saline liquid out of which it arose, and into which in due course it will some day return. 'We feel that we are greater than we know.' Or, reversing the metaphor, we might liken our present state to that of the hulls of ships submerged in a dim ocean among strange beasts, propelled in a blind manner through space; proud, perhaps, of accumulating many barnacles of decoration; only recognizing our destination by bumping against the dock wall; and with no cognizance of the deck, and the cabins, and spars and the sails, no thought of the sextant and the compass and the captain, no perception of the lookout on the mast, of the distant horizon, no vision of objects far ahead, dangers to be avoided, destinations to be reached, other ships to be spoken with by other means than bodily contact—a region of sunshine and cloud, of space, of perception, and of intelligence, utterly inaccessible to the parts below the water line."

There has been much confusion caused to the student of The New Psychology by the various terms employed by many of its writers, particularly in connection with these "out-of-conscious" mental states and regions. Many of the earlier authorities place in one group all the phenomena and activities of the several regions beyond and below the plane of consciousness. This plan causes much confusion because the several attributes attributed to these "subjective," "subconscious," or "subliminal" minds, as they are called, are diametrically opposed to each other, and the beginner is soon enmeshed in a web of incompatible facts, theories and ideas. But of late years there has been a disposition of teachers and writers to observe the classification first observed by some of the Oriental teachers many centuries ago, and at present there is generally recognized that there are *two* general "out-of-conscious" regions of planes of the minds (with various sub-planes) which are known as the "subconscious" and "super-conscious" regions, planes or "minds," respectively. Some good teachers and writers still adhere to the old classification, "conscious" and "subconscious," respectively, placing in the latter all of the "out-of-conscious" phenomena, high and low, but the tendency is in the other direction. You will notice in the quotations that we have given in this chapter that the majority of the authorities recognize the "above-conscious" as well as the "below-conscious" planes or regions of the mind. In the next two chapters we shall consider these two planes or regions, in some detail.

What is called the "field of consciousness" or "conscious mind" is really but a very small part of the mental kingdom of the Ego. It is used to receive the report of the senses; to examine, analyze, combine, and use the stored-up material of the subconscious as it is brought into the field of consciousness in some degree of order and system; to perform the work of the reason; to choose or decide; to put into operation the will, and in similar ways. It is the great mental "clearing house" where alone certain mental work may be performed. It is the eye-piece of the mental microscope or telescope. It is the great "clearing" of the mind into which pass the things of the jungle, woods and canyons, as well as the things coming down from the mountains of the mind. It may be thought of as a spot in the mental area, illuminated by the bright light of consciousness, whereby and wherein the Ego may examine, decide upon, choose and act upon the various mental images, ideas, feelings, etc., that are brought before it for consideration and judgment. It is the Open Court of the Mind.

From the field of consciousness are passed into the subconscious region many experiences that are to be stored away for the future use of the individual and the race, which experiences afterward are reproduced in that field of the individual or of the race, as feelings, emotions, memories, thoughts, ideas or other mental material. Into the field of consciousness also pass many new things from the higher, or superconscious regions—flashes of inspiration, genius, intuition and other higher mental material. By keeping this picture of the higher and lower planes of "out-of-consciousness" before you, you will be enabled to understand much that has heretofore been dark and confusing. It is of the greatest importance to keep the field of consciousness clean and in good condition, and to keep its chief instruments, the Attention and the

The New Psychology

Intellect, in good working order. But at the same time to regard it as the *only* region of the mind is a great mistake, and amounts to depriving yourself of certain knowledge much needed by you. The New Psychology covers *all* the regions of the mind, conscious and "out-of-conscious"—giving to each its place, and to each its employment and use. It is an "all-around" science as well as an "up-to-date" one.

Chapter V.

The Subconscious.

As we have said, The New Psychology concerns itself to a marked degree with the activities of the subconscious region of the mind. instead of regarding these activities as abnormal and worthy only of scientific interest, it knows and teaches that in this region of the mind the greater part of the mentative work is performed, and that work of great value may be produced by an intelligent ordering of the subconscious activities. It is in this difference in the consideration of these faculties, activities and capabilities that The New Psychology differs radically from the old psychology. A new field of thought, work and activity is opened out to every individual when he is made acquainted with the subconscious region of mentation and its laws. In this connection we must ask you to note the distinction made in this work between the subconscious region or plane, and the superconscious. The subconscious plane is *below* the field of consciousness—the superconscious plane is *above* the conscious field.

To many students of popular metaphysics "new thought," and the newer views of psychology, the subconscious plane of mind, or the "subconscious mind" as it is usually called in the popular 'Works, is usually regarded as something spiritual, extraordinary, soulful, mystic—something having properties and qualities far beyond the ordinary mind. But The New Psychology does not so hold—although it admits the existence of a superconscious region or plane of mind which has activities which may be considered supernormal and unusual. To The New Psychology the subconscious mind is simply the plane or region of the mind in which is stored up a great variety of impressions from the past of the individual and of the race. In that region of the mind is to be found those strange impressions which have come down to us through the ages of time—the inheritances of the race, which manifest as "instinct" and instinctive feeling. Many things that were experienced by our ancestors come down to us in the shape of impressions that are reproduced in the field of consciousness with more or less clearness, as opportunity demands. Our "feelings," likes and dislikes, prejudices, tastes, inclinations, and other mental states which rise up to the field of consciousness from time to time—the mental qualities which are in our subconsciousness from our birth—come to us in this way. The individual has the benefit of all the experience of the race acquired through the ages, the essence of which is impressed upon his subconscious mentality. Besides this each individual has a certain "natural character" which is his from birth, and by reason of direct inheritance, which is also impressed upon his subconscious mentality. It is true, very true, that the individual may alter and radically change this natural character by the methods of The New Psychology, but the fact remains that the individual has a certain natural character of his own, independent of his training. Every one has his or her own natural tastes and preferences, likes and dislikes; character; nature. Every mother of a large family knows that no two children of the little brood has the same disposition or nature. Every teacher knows that each child has its particular personality. Every individual has his own personality. And the things that go to make up that particular personality are the impressions contained in the subconscious plane of the mind.

The Subconscious

But these inherited impressions are only a part of the material of that wondrous mental storehouse. From the time that the child is able to recognize the outer world, it begins acquiring new impressions, all of which are duly recorded in the subconsciousness. Each little bit of experience gained by the conscious mind is then passed on to the subconscious region—is impressed upon the mental phonographic records of that region. The depth and clearness of the impression depends upon the degree of attention and interest bestowed upon the original subject or object that produced the impressions. The things that interest us attract the greater degree of attention, and the greater the degree of attention the deeper and clearer the subconscious impression. You see then, that *this subconscious region of the mind is something very similar to that which we have called Memory—only that it occupies a larger field and has greater activities than those formerly attributed to memory.* The faculty or activities that we call "memory" are simply a portion of a greater field—a Greater Memory—that we call the subconscious region of the mind. By bearing this in mind you will be able to form a much clearer idea of the subconscious plane.

In addition to the above stated kind of impressions, the subconsciousness contains records of many things that have been suggested to the person and then allowed to pass unchallenged to the subconscious storehouse. We believe in many things without question, and accept them as truth, which have never been subjected to the scrutiny of our reasoning faculties or judgment. We have swallowed them whole, just because we heard some one say them with an air of authority, or else read them in the same way; or perhaps we heard them repeated so often that we took it for granted they were true; or else we saw that everyone else seemed to believe and accept them, and we followed the custom. A little self-examination will startle anyone at the revelations along this line. Very few things have been submitted to reason or judgment. It is so much easier to take them in the capsule of authority, custom, or repetition. And after we have so accepted them, and particularly after we have acquiesced a number of times in their verity, we will claim them as our very own and will defend them vigorously and will resent any attack upon their virtue and validity—just as if we had originally thought them all out and submitted them to the scrutiny of our reason. Those of us who have felt compelled to throw out from our minds some of these "cuckoo-eggs" of thought, will realize fully how much attached we had become to these false-children of our minds, and how much distress it caused us to show them the mental door after having entertained them so long as our very own. The subconsciousness is very full of this class of impressions.

Another class of impressions is contained in this subconscious region—the impressions of habit. We know how we may acquire the habit of performing tasks, difficult at first, until at last we are able to do them "without thinking." The piano player, the operator of the typewriter, the sewing machine operator, the telegrapher, the typesetter, and many other performers of tasks, know that while at first they had to watch each step of the work, and guard every motion, they gradually became more expert until at last they were able to perform the task with a minimum of attention, and often while a portion of their mind was occupied in thinking of something entirely different. The subconsciousness has taken over the task, and performs it almost automatically.

We must not overlook the fact that the subconsciousness also contains the impressions that manifest in the operation of the physical functions of the body, which are almost altogether performed involuntarily and along subconscious lines. The heart beats without our knowledge, consciousness, or volition. While we may take over the process of breathing, the greater part of this work of respiration is performed subconsciously and involuntarily. The work of digestion, the circulation, and the thousand and one other functions of the body are performed without reference to the consciousness. It is only when something goes wrong that the conscious mind becomes aware that the internal organs are there. All this work is a part of the subconscious activities. But remember this, that in the course of evolution each of these automatic and involuntary movements and actions was learned by experience, and after being mastered by our earlier progenitors was then passed on to the region of the subconscious—the race memory—in a manner similar to that whereby we pass on the acts of walking, piano-playing and other acquired physical movements. The subconsciousness is a busy place—a hive of industry.

For, remember this, that although we have spoken of it as merely a great storehouse of race-memories, and individual-memories (in the broad sense) yet it is more than a storehouse devoid of activities. It is filled with active working faculties and mental machinery. As we have said elsewhere, the activities of the subconscious region forcibly remind one of a workshop filled with active, earnest, faithful tiny workers, willing and anxious to do the work of the individual, if they are only told what is needed. And it is in directing these tiny workers of the subconscious mind that The New Psychology becomes so useful to the student. Not content with simply allowing the subconscious to store away impressions, and then to reproduce only those absolutely necessary to the ordinary mind, it teaches that a high degree of activity may be encouraged in that region, and thereby the individual's efficiency to himself and to the community may be greatly increased.

You see, then, that the subconscious region contains only that which has been placed in it by the race, or the individual. It originates nothing new, although it can be used to form countless new combinations of its materials, and thus perform wonderful creative work for its owner. By the use of the imagination the subconscious region may be made to unfold great stores of material, arranged in orderly system, and capable of being grouped together in new and strange combinations—

this is Invention. The so-called "higher powers" of the mind are not to be found in the subconscious region—they belong to the superconscious plane, as we shall see in the next chapter. In this connection we think it well to state an idea of our own, which is not mentioned generally in writings or teachings along these lines. We allude to the possession of certain lower forms of unusual "psychic" power by some persons, which forms lack the elements of the so-called "higher powers" just alluded to, but still are outside of the ordinary forms of sense-impressions—by some these phases of phenomena are called the "lower psychic faculties." The persons possessing and manifesting these "powers" are often far from being advanced spiritually, mentally, or morally, and this fact has surprised and perplexed many of the investigators of the subject. This class of phenomena differs materially from that of the superconsciousness, and evidently belongs to a lower plane—and yet to what plane? Not to consciousness, surely, and if the subconsciousness is merely a record of race impressions and individual experiences, etc., how can these phenomena be credited to it? We have thought it likely that these "lower psychic" activities *may be the result of faculties formerly exercised by the race, but since discarded in the course of evolution, and now found only as "vestigal" remnants in some of the race.* This view finds corroboration in a study of the mental activities of the lower animals, and primitive races of man, in both of which we find evidences of "sensing" other than those manifested by man. The animals and lower races have a sense of smell almost abnormal to civilized man, and they may have, and seem to have, other means of "sensing" objects. If this be true, then each of us must have some record of these discarded senses in our subconsciousness, which in some cases give rise to those instances of strange "awareness" noted in certain people, and which belong to the class of the "lower psychic" phenomena, as distinguished from the "higher psychic" phenomena belonging to the class of genius, intuition, spirituality, etc. We do not insist upon this theory—it is merely

The Subconscious

a conjecture, offered for what it may be worth. It certainly seems to "fill in" a gap in the study of abnormal psychology.

Let us now pass on to the region of the superconscious—the higher planes of the mind.

Chapter VI.

The Superconscious.

It is difficult to explain The New Psychology conception of the superconscious plane of mind, without approaching perilously near the border line that separates psychology from metaphysics and philosophy. Even escaping this danger, we are compelled to use the terms of evolution as used in the science of biology.

In the first place, instead of being the Greater Memory, or storehouse of the impressions of the past, as is the case with the subconsciousness, the superconsciousness of the individual is the latent possibilities of the future man, or superman. And the flashes from this region that occasionally reach the field of consciousness are practically the prophecies of the future of the race. That which is now the superconscious region of the individual will some day become the ordinary plane of every-day mentation of the advanced race. The superconsciousness is the consciousness of the future individuals of the race, and in it are stored the latent faculties and mental activities of a higher race of beings. To some favored ones of the present race there come flashes from this wonderful region of the mind, and we call them "genius," "inspiration," "intuition," and other terms denoting higher and uncommon mental activities and states.

The New Psychology

In each individual there is stored this great reservoir of future mental development—why, or how, we do not know—but that they *are* we do know. Just as the oak tree dwells latent within the acorn; just as the coming Shakespeare, Milton, Darwin or Spencer was at one time latent within a single cell; So are these latent faculties and powers in the mind of each and every individual, awaiting the stroke of the clock of evolutionary unfoldment. And when these flashes pass down into the field of consciousness, we recognize them as coming from *above*, and not from *below*.

The mental evolution of the race is not alone a matter of growth in the sense of addition—it is in the nature of the *unfoldment* of the latent qualities, faculties, and powers inherent in the mind, or perhaps the unfoldment into expression of some inherent power or quality of the Ego. At any rate it is undoubtedly an unfoldment—a revealing of something that had been hidden away from sight and expression. The child, in a few years, passes over the stages of mental evolution that the race required centuries to attain—this is the work of the subconsciousness. And the man of to-day is slowly, laboriously, but surely unfolding into greater and grander mental states and activities. Mental growth comes not alone from without—there is an inner urge constantly at work, pressing ever on toward higher and greater things. There is always this dual expression—the attraction of the mind toward outer objects which stimulate and hasten its expression, and the inner urge constantly pressing it forward. It has been well claimed that there can be no progress without the outer things to attract and interest the mind and to cause it to grow by exercise and use. But it is likewise true that there would be, and could be, no growth unless there was something to respond to the outer and to force it to unfold. There is the evolutionary urge, as well as the evolutionary pull of attraction.

And so, this is what we mean by the superconsciousness—the higher regions of the mind that are beginning to unfold into a greater and more glorious consciousness. That this unfoldment

The Superconscious

will bring to the race new senses, new channels of "awareness," cannot be doubted. Just as from mere sensation the present states of consciousness arose—just as from a crude sense of feeling the wonderful sense of seeing sprang into existence—so from the comparatively crude senses of "awareness" of outside objects that we possess to-day will undoubtedly unfold senses that transcend even our wildest flights of imagination to-day. There seems to be good reason for believing that space will be practically annihilated to the beings of the future. Just as the sense of seeing is an improved form of feeling, so will there undoubtedly come a sense of perception that will be a highly improved sense of seeing. And, more than this, the sense of cognizance and awareness of the thoughts of others—the "telepathy" or "telementation" of to-day-will undoubtedly be a common possession of the race in the future, a fact that will revolutionize life as we know it. For when the thoughts of all become as an open book to all, then will pass away deceit, falsity, hypocrisy, untruth, and all the rest. Higher standards of life will be demanded and maintained, and the interests of all will be identified and identical. With a common thought arising from the "circulation of thought" there will come a common interest and aim to the race. In the recognition of these latent faculties, even now beginning to show signs of unfoldment, there is to be found a sane basis for the expectation of the coming of many things that now are held to belong to "the millennium."

But it is not of the future that we wish to speak—our work is in the present. From these higher regions of the mind are coming to the race not only the expression of genius, inspiration and intuition, but also the consciousness of relationship between all men—all living things. With a dawning consciousness of this relationship, men naturally feel nearer to each other, and to the universe, and consequently express themselves differently. The feeling of kindness, sympathy, brotherhood and general tolerance that is coming to the race arises from the flashes from these higher regions of the mind. These things are not obtained through the intellect, they are a matter of consciousness, of higher feeling. And this consciousness and feeling certainly do not arise from the lower regions of the mind, for the past was not concerned with these things of the future. Many of the things that come into our minds, that we are apt to think "came from *above*" really do come from above—from the higher regions of the mind—the superconsciousness.

That the race is unfolding into a new plane of "sensing," and in to a new field of "knowing" and thinking, cannot be doubted by any one who studies the signs of the times. In the first case, we are obtaining accurate and reliable reports of super-normal sensing in isolated cases from the scientific societies organized to study psychical phenomena. We have evidences of a higher form of "awareness at a distance" which for want of a better name is known as "clairvoyance," a name, by the way, that has unpleasant associations by reason of its use by many charlatans and tricksters. The evidence in support of these phenomena is too voluminous and trustworthy to be brushed lightly aside. The records are full of well authenticated instances occurring to persons of the highest standing and character. And the evidence in favor of "thought transference" is even stronger— for that matter there are but few people to-day who have not had a personal experience along these lines.

Many have been prejudiced against these phenomena for the reason that they have considered them to be used as a proof of supernatural powers, etc. But there is nothing supernatural about it. No doubt the sense of sight came slowly to the lower forms of life—certainly it came late in the history of the earth's living forms. And if these lower forms had been able to think about it they would have been prejudiced in the beginning against the reports of the few of their number who claimed to be able to "feel things at a distance"—for that is what seeing really is, a developed sense of feeling the impact of the light waves. And no doubt these lower forms would have organized Societies for Psychical Research, amid the sneers of the non-seeing brethren, until finally the sense of seeing became common to the race. And there is no reason whatever for holding that the evolution of the senses has ceased its operations. There is far more reason for thinking that there will be many new senses unfolded to the race-senses for receiving impressions of electric waves, magnetic waves, thought-waves, and other waves not now sensed by the mind.

If we could sense the waves of electricity or magnetism, a new world would be opened up for us. And, as we have said, a sensing of thought-waves would revolutionize the world. Just imagine what the universe would seem to the race were it devoid of the sense of sight, or of hearing. And think what it would mean to have two more senses of equal importance opened to it. Our present senses touch the universe at only a very small segment of its whole. Each new sense opens up a new universe. As Isaac Taylor well said: "Perhaps within the field occupied by the visible and ponderable universe there is existing and moving another element fraught with other species of life—corporeal, indeed, and various in its orders, but not open to the cognizance of those who are confined to the conditions of animal organization....Is it to be thought that the eye of man is the measure of the Creator's power?—and has He created nothing which He has not exposed to our senses? The contrary seems much more than barely possible; ought we not to think it almost certain?" And as Masson has said: "If a new sense or two were added to the present normal number in man, that which is now the phenomenal world for all of us might, for all we know, burst into something amazingly wider and different, in consequence of the additional revelations through these new senses."

The student must free his mind from the error that there is anything unnatural or "miraculous" in the idea of additional senses unfolding to the race. Every sense is a "miracle," if these new ones be so considered. What could be more miraculous than the sense of sight—or still more, to the sense of sight aided as it is by the microscope and the telescope which but heighten the normal power? To think that we can "sense" what is going on in the universe of a drop of water, or changes on a distant planet—is not this a miracle? Is not the fact that you, who are reading this page, can "know" the shapes of these letters on the page, at a distance, and with no bodily contact—is not this a miracle? In our chapter on Impressions you may see that all the senses are but forms of "feeling" the impressions coming from outside objects—that we *do not* see, feel, hear, smell, or taste the objects themselves, but merely the impressions reaching the brain from these objects—messages along the nerves that are then translated by our brains. Can anyone knowing these facts claim to know or believe that there are not other avenues whereby these impressions may reach us, particularly when we know that each one of the present five avenues of the senses were slowly evolved or unfolded as Life climbed the scale of evolution. Let us be fair in this matter, and while reserving the right to question, examine and determine the validity of any and all claims of super-normal sensing, still maintain the open mind toward the subject.

And not only in the direction of sensing does the superconsciousness hold improvement for the race. In the realm of reason there is every right to believe that new faculties will be unfolded, just as the present faculties were unfolded in the past. One has but to study man in the scale of reasoning ability, to understand that there is an evolutionary scale of reason in both the race as a whole, and between individuals—not even considering the lower animals. Is it not reasonable to believe that the man of the future will be as far ahead of the average man of our race and time, as the latter is ahead of the African Bushman or Digger Indian? Have we reached the limits of thought and reason? History and science answer this question, in no uncertain tones, in the negative. Have we not had examples in the scattered instances of geniuses of giant mental power—forerunners of the men to come?

The Superconscious

In the superconscious regions of the mind lie the seeds and germs of these future senses and reasoning powers—latent, awaiting the call of unfoldment. And from that region comes all that is best, and highest, and greatest in our mental activities to-day. And by recognizing this fact and opening up the mind toward this higher self, we invite and make welcome these messages from above—and encourage their coming. And thus do we grow and unfold.

Chapter VII.

Impressions.

It is difficult for one to realize how dependent the mind is upon the impressions received from the outside world through the channels of the senses. Perhaps the only way that we are able to realize the importance of these outside impressions is to imagine our condition were we deprived of them. As Halleck has well said: "Suppose a child of intelligent parents were ushered into the world without a nerve leading from his otherwise perfect brain to any portion of his body, with no optic nerve to transmit the glorious sensations from the eye, no auditory nerve to conduct the vibrations of the mother's voice, no tactile nerves to convey the touch of a hand, no olfactory nerve to rouse the brain with the delicate aroma from the orchards and the wild flowers in spring, no gustatory, thermal or muscular nerves. Could such a child live, as the years rolled on, the books of Shakespeare and of Milton would be opened in vain before the child's eyes. The wisest men might talk to him with utmost eloquence, all to no purpose. Nature could not whisper one of her inspiring truths into his deaf ear, could not light up that dark mind with a picture of the rainbow or of a human face. No matter how perfect might be the child's brain and his inherited capacity for mental activities, his faculties would remain for this life shrouded in Egyptian darkness. Perception could give memory nothing to retain, and thought could not weave her matchless fabrics without materials." Carpenter says: "If it were possible for a human being to come into the world with a brain perfectly prepared to be the instrument of psychical operations, but with all the inlets to sensations closed, we have every reason to believe that the mind would remain dormant like a seed buried in the earth." Stewart says: "That the powers of the understanding would forever continue dormant were it not for the action of things external on the bodily frame, is a proposition now universally admitted by philosophers." Helmholtz says: "Apprehension by the senses supplies directly or indirectly the material of all human knowledge, or at least the stimulus necessary to develop every inborn faculty of the mind." Virchow says: "Even the highest ideas are slowly and gradually developed from the accumulation of sense experiences, and their truth is only guaranteed by the possibility of finding concrete examples for them in real existence." Carpenter again says: "The activity of the mind is just as much the result of its consciousness of external impressions, by which its faculties are called into play, as the life of the body is dependent upon the appropriation of nutrient materials and the constant influence of external forces." Maudsley says: "As we perceive more accurately, so we remember more correctly, judge more soundly, and imagine more truly." And as Kay says: "The senses are the means by which the mind obtains its knowledge of the outside world. Shut out from all direct communication with the outer world, it knows, and can know, nothing of what exists or is passing there, except what comes to it through the senses. Its knowledge of what is external to itself is therefore dependent upon the number, state, and condition of the sensory organs."

It is true that the above authorities speak from the standpoint of the old psychology, and ignore the evidences of the dawning phases of consciousness from the superconscious plane. But even so, what they say of the senses will apply to any other senses or channels of impressions which may be evolved in man. The Ego can receive impressions from outside only through the channels of some kind of sense organism, be those senses physical, "psychic" or spiritual. With all the channels closed the Ego must remain with all its powers latent and unexpressed—knowing nothing beyond its own existence. It is a wonderful thought this idea of the Ego dwelling within the individual mind, with its organ of the brain, and its wonderful nervous system over which it receives the messages of the senses from the outside universe, those impressions to be stored away in the subconscious regions of the mind, thence to reappear in recollection, imagination, and thought, after being weighed, arranged, grouped, and valued by the reason.

These channels of impression from the outside world—the senses—are generally said to be five in number-viz.: Feeling, Seeing, Hearing, Smelling and Tasting. Some authorities substitute the sense of "Touch" for that of Feeling, and add to the list the various feelings of the muscular system such as the perception of weight, etc.; the feelings of thirst, hunger, etc., and the various feelings of the internal organs. But this is a distinction without a difference for these things, and touch, are but forms of Feeling. So far as the internal feelings are concerned, we are not called upon to notice them in this connection, for our inquiry is regarding the impressions from the outer world received by the Ego. As Bernstein says: "The characteristic difference between these common sensations and the sensations of the senses is that by the latter we gain knowledge of the occurrences and objects which belong to the external world, and that we refer the sensations which they produce to external objects, whilst by the former we only feel conditions of our own body."

A close analysis of the various sense-impressions confirms the theory of the ancient Greek philosopher, Democritus, promulgated over two thousand years ago, to the effect that all

The New Psychology

the senses are but modifications and refinements of the original sense of touch or feeling. Feeling was the first sense to appear in the scale of evolution, and the others have evolved from it. To understand this we must realize that all impressions made upon the organs of sense arise from the motion of material particles from outside coming in contact with sensitive portions of the physical organism of the individual, and setting up nerve activities which affect the brain. As Morrell says: "The only way the external world affects the nervous system is by means of motion. Light is motion; sound is motion; heat is motion; touch is motion; taste and smell are motion. The world is known to sense simply by virtue of, and in relation to, the motions of its particles. These motions are appreciated and continued by the nervous system, and by it are brought at length to the mind's perception....The last material action we can trace in every process of sensation previous to its entering the abode of consciousness is motion." And as Kay says: "Whatever acts upon an organ of sense does so in the form of motion. Nothing can act upon the senses or be taken up by them unless it present itself to them in the form of motion." And these various forms of motion of the particles of matter—the vibrations of these particles—are recognized by the sensitive "feeling" of the organs of the eye, the ear, the nostrils, the tongue, and the skin. It is all feeling, from touch to seeing.

You look at this page, seeing the white paper and the little black letters of the print. You imagine that in some mysterious way there is some connection between the paper and ink and your "sight"—there is, but not just in the way you imagine. There is no subtle and mysterious connection. What happens is this: the light striking the page is reflected to the eye and produces a corresponding *image* on the retina of the eye—all this is physical and has nothing to do with the mind, for the lens of a camera will catch the image just as does the retina of the eye. But here is where the mental process occurs—this image upon the retina is caused by waves of light—light vibrations—which,

Impressions

impinging upon the delicate and sensitive nerves of the eye, are *felt* there and by the brain. The seeing is really *feeling* of a very delicate kind—feeling of the light-wave vibrations. In the same way the ear catches the sound vibrations and the tympanum is caused to vibrate in unison—just as does the diaphragm of a phonograph—and the nerves of the ear *feel* these delicate vibrations. Smelling is but the *feeling*, by the nerves of the mucous membrane of the nostrils, of the tiny particles of gaseous matter arising from the cause of the odor. Taste is but a fine sense of feeling the vibratory and chemical action of the particles of food, etc., by the taste-nerves of the mouth and tongue aided by the other nerves of feeling of that region. And more than this, the translation of the *feeling* into the knowing is not complete until the impression is transmitted over the nervous system to the brain where the *feeling* is actually experienced and is translated into "knowing" by the mystery of the presence of the Ego. Cut the nerves, and no sensation is felt when the light-waves, or sound-waves or other waves producing sensation beat upon the organs. At the last the *feeling* that we call seeing, touching, smelling, tasting and hearing is completed, even physically, only when the brain receives the impressions and *feels* them. What occurs then is beyond the knowledge of man. In some wonderful way the feeling is transmuted into consciousness—the Ego *knows* certain things of the non-ego, or outside world. How the Ego accomplishes this is a mystery wrapped up in the greater mystery of the Ego itself. We can do no more than to echo the thoughtful statement of Huxley, the eminent scientist, who said: "How it is that anything so remarkable as a state of consciousness comes about by the result of irritating nervous tissue, is just as unaccountable as the presence of the jinnee when Aladdin rubbed his lamp."

And so, we must rest content with a general understanding of the mechanism whereby the Ego establishes communication with the outside world, Dwelling alone in calm solitude the Ego is constantly receiving the messages from without its dwelling place, as well as from the different rooms of its own place of abode. Telegraph and telephone lines run into that central office, from all directions—telescopes and other optical appliances are trained to all points—heat-registering, light-registering, sound-registering, and motion-registering instruments are at hand and in constant use. All these instruments have been furnished by Nature for the use of the Ego—or shall we say that the Ego itself fashioned them to meet its requirements? Who can tell this thing? At any rate, the fact remains that the wonderful instruments that the intellect and ingenuity of man have been able to fashion after centuries of experiment are but extensions or imitations of these instruments of Nature—the lens of the eye, the tympanum of the ear, the telegraphic wires of the nerves, the analytical nerves of the taste and smell, the heat registering nerves of the skin, and all the rest. The term "Nature" is but a veil concealing, and yet revealing, the Something within Nature—the "nature" of Nature.

And remember this always—that it is the Ego who sees; the Ego who feels; the Ego who smells; the Ego who tastes; the Ego who hears—and not the organs to which we generally ascribe these qualities. And if in the evolution of the race, or the individual, there appear other and higher organs whereby man may receive newer and fuller impressions from the outside world, it will always be the Ego who senses through them; who is made "aware" by reason of them; who *knows* through them. The Ego is the Real Self, the Real "I," the Real Individual. Strip from it its instruments of sense—its cloak of personality—it will still remain *itself*, something different from all else, something apart, under, and back of all; *sui generis*;—the "I."

Chapter VIII.

Perception.

IN OUR chapter on Impressions, we have seen that it is always the Ego who "perceives" the impression registered by the nerves of the organs of sense. The organs receive, the nerves transmit, the brain registers; but it is always the Ego who *perceives*. But, be this remembered, the Ego does not always perceive the messages from the outside world with equal degrees of clearness—sometimes it does not receive them at all. Perception is a matter of volition with the Ego—a matter dependent upon the will. The Ego may will to give its *attention* to a message from the senses, or it may refuse to do so—it may will to give the strongest degree of attention, or it may decide to give but scant attention to the message. At first this may seem to be an extreme statement, and it may seem difficult to believe that a man possessing the normal sense of hearing could escape hearing the report of a gun, whether he willed to do so or not. It is true that in ordinary instances, provided the will offers no obstacle, the amount of voluntary attention requisite for perceiving the sound of the report of a gun would be very small—so small as to be almost worthy of the name of "involuntary attention." But, on the other hand, there are instances of men who were so concentrated on other tasks that they failed to hear the noise of the cannon of a whole army, and only realized that a battle had occurred in the neighborhood, after it was all over. In the same way men have failed to feel a severe wound by reason of concentrated attention being directed elsewhere. And it is a well-proven psychological fact that there have been men who were able to inhibit pain by an effort of the will. The Attention is a matter of the employment of the will of the Ego. Interest attracts the attention and relieves the will of much of its work in the direction of holding the attention upon the object or idea. The art of attention may be cultivated by practice under the direction of the will.

All the authorities upon psychology, old and new, agree upon the importance of the cultivation of the attention in the direction of perception. The better under control the attention is, the clearer the perception; and the clearer the perception the deeper are the impressions received, and the greater their number and detail. As Kay says: "The greater one's power of attention, the longer and more steadily he is able to fix it upon a subject, the better will he be able to follow out the same train of thought, and the greater will be the amount of success attending his labors. It is this power of attention,—this power of keeping a particular object before the mind till he has thoroughly mastered it, that more than anything else distinguishes the man of genius from others. Indeed it is said that 'possibly the most comprehensive definition of genius is the power of concentrating and prolonging the attention upon any one subject.'" Newton said: "I keep a subject continually before me, and wait till the first dawning opens slowly by little and little into a clear light. If I have made any improvements in the sciences, it is owing more to patient attention than to any other talent." Brodie said: "The mind that possesses the faculty of Attention in the greatest degree of perfection, will take cognizance of relations of which another mind has no perception." And glancing at the opposite side of the question, we see that in imbeciles, idiots and others of impaired mentality, the faculty of attention is very deficient. As Esquirol says: "Imbeciles and idiots are destitute of the faculty of attention." And a medical authority says that: "The growing deficiency of attention points to a coming imbecility, and especially to an impending attack of softening of the brain." Attention, being dependent upon the direct use of the will, is the mark of a trained mind and strong individuality; the reverse being true of those deficient in this faculty.

There are records of individuals who have developed their attention to a degree almost incredible—and all by practice. Houdin, the celebrated conjurer of France, developed his almost miraculous degree of attention by practicing before the shop-windows, taking a long glance, and then trying to recall what he had seen. At first he was able to recall only a few things,—because he had *perceived* only a few things. But as he practiced steadily he improved so that he could recall quite a number of articles. He persevered and practiced until finally he was able to perceive and recall the majority of the contents of an average shop-window after taking a single glance at it. In explaining the process, Houdin said: "For instance, I can safely assert that a lady seeing another pass at full speed in a carriage, will have had time to analyze her toilette from her bonnet to her shoes, and be able to describe not only the fashion and quality of the stuffs; but also to say whether the lace be real or only machine made. I have known ladies to do this."

Specialists in various lines have so trained their attention that they are able to see scores of minute details of an object in a hasty glance. A well known college professor was said to be able to read a quarter page of an ordinary book at a single glance. Musicians "take in" a great number of bars to be played, by a glance at the page of music. It is all a matter of interest, will, and practice. It is astonishing how little we "perceive" of the many things we "see." Halleck gives an interesting account of this, saying: "A body may be imaged on the retina without insuring perception. There must be an effort to concentrate the attention upon the many things which the world presents to our senses. A man once said to the pupils of a large school, all of whom had often seen cows: 'I should like to find out how many of you know whether a cow's ears are above, below, behind or in front of her horns. I want only those pupils to raise their hands who are sure about the position and who will promise to give a dollar to charity if they answer wrong." Only two hands were raised. Their owners had drawn cows and in order to do that had been forced to concentrate their attention upon the animals. Fifteen pupils were sure that they had seen cats climb trees and descend them. There was unanimity of opinion that the cat went up head first. When asked whether the cats came down head or tail first, the majority were sure that the cats descended as they were never known to do. Anyone who had ever noticed the shape of the claws of any beast of prey could have answered that question without seeing an actual descent."

In view of the fact that the subconscious mentality is filled with the impressions received by reason of the direction of the attention, it becomes important that we learn to manage that faculty of the mind so that we may employ it to our well-being and advancement. An intelligent use of the attention consists in the voluntary direction and concentration of the faculty upon objects or ideas which one's clear and cool judgment may decide to be conducive to his development, progress and well-being. This applies not only to the employment of the attention toward outside objects, but also in the matter of inward contemplation, retrospection, and meditation. Not only may we develop the positive and desirable qualities of the mind by directing our attention upon the appropriate and proper things of the outside world, but we may also deepen the effect of the positive ideas by turning the attention upon them often, thus deepening the original impression and increasing the dynamic force of the ideas. And as we may develop the positive qualities in this way, so may we neutralize the effect of negative things and thoughts by refusing to allow the attention to dwell upon them.

Attention is divided by psychologists into two general classes, involuntary and voluntary. Involuntary attention is that form of attention which is directed to any passing object with little or no exercise of the will; while voluntary attention is that form of attention in which there is an active employment of the will in directing the attention, and then holding it fixed upon objects approved of by the judgment of the individual. Voluntary attention is one of the marks of the trained mind, and the control of the involuntary attention is its usual accompaniment. The untrained mind manifests little or no voluntary attention, and finds it difficult to concentrate upon a task; but in such cases the involuntary attention is active, and the attention is attracted by every trifling occurrence. Persons lacking in voluntary attention find it difficult to master any subject, or to study any object or question. They are constantly being "side-tracked" by every foolish object that presents itself. Such people are at the mercy of every passing object or thought. The young child has but little or no voluntary attention, but its involuntary attention is strongly in evidence. It is attracted by every moving trifle, for the moment, and yet finds it difficult to fasten its attention upon the printed page of the lesson. It is only by systematic training that it is able to acquire the study-habit, and often even then only to a limited degree. The men and women in every walk of life who have accomplished things have possessed strong powers of voluntary attention.

There are three general laws governing the voluntary employment of the attention. They are as follows:

I. Attention follows Interest; and Interest follows Attention. Interest in an object makes it easier to fasten the attention upon it—lack of interest renders the task doubly difficult. But by using the attention to examine the details and little points of an object, we often succeed in building up and creating a new interest. An understanding of this paradox makes one the master of the handling of uninteresting objects by the mind. First examine the object until you create an interest; then the interest will make renewed attention pleasant, and thus will new interest be created, and so on, like an endless chain.

II. Attention diminishes in quality and degree unless the object varies in stimulus; or unless new qualities or attributes of interest are developed in it. That is to say, unless the object possesses changing features, or unless we are able to discover some new points of interest in it, the attention tires, weakens and wavers. Therefore it is important that the attention be relieved by viewing objects from new standpoints, and that new interest be added in any possible way. Change of attention means rest for the attention. Avoid getting into ruts in employing the attention—constant variation, combination and change of viewpoints are great aids.

III. Unrelieved attention diminishes in constancy. Therefore relieve the faculty by shutting it off from the particular object that has tired it, and by giving it other things to consider—something entirely different. Or else allow it to manifest on the involuntary plane, and "play" on things of trifling importance, for the sake of the rest. Constantly holding the attention upon one set of ideas or objects tends to tire it and impair its efficiency. Minds, as well as bodies, require games, play, recreation and relaxation. Learn not only to direct and hold the attention upon any object or idea, but also to detach it and hold it from the "one-idea," or one thing that has overworked it. Give your attention a vacation trip, or a half-holiday, and it will return to work refreshed and with renewed vigor. Have outside "side-lines" of interest in which to plunge the attention and thus relieve it from its work on the main idea. Concentrated attention, used intelligently, works miracles of accomplishment, and produces giants of mentality; but used without rule or mastery it produces abnormal results and evolves "cranks," fanatics and monomaniacs. Use the mind, but do not let it use

Perception
you. In this as in everything, else, be the master and not the slave.

Chapter IX.

Mental Paths.

There is a tendency of the mind to tread the beaten paths of mental activity. It is always easier to do a thing the second time—to think the thought again—to follow a mental path once traveled over. And the oftener we tread the old path, the easier does it become to go over it again. Unless under the direct control of the will, the mind follows the line of the least resistance, and consequently it instinctively moves toward the old path. This tendency is the cause of that which we know as "habit." Habit is at the same time the greatest blessing, and yet the greatest curse to man. Desirable habits cultivated give the character a bent in the right direction, and render the proper course the easiest, and consequently the one instinctively selected. But, for the same reason, bad habits make it easier for the person to follow the mental path created by them. Therefore the formation of mental paths becomes an important matter, and one upon which The New Psychology lays special stress.

Dumont has well expressed this truth when he says: "Every one knows how a garment, after having been worn a certain time, clings to the shape of the body better than when it was new; there has been a change in the tissue, and this change is a new habit of cohesion. A lock works better after being used some time; at the outset more force was required to overcome certain roughness in the mechanism. The overcoming the resistance is a phenomenon of habit. It is less trouble to fold a paper when it has been folded already; and just so in the nervous system the impressions of outer objects fashion for themselves more and more appropriate paths, and these vital phenomena recur under similar excitements from without when they have been interrupted for a certain time." Maudsley says: "If an act became no easier after being done several times, if the careful direction of consciousness were necessary to its accomplishment on each occasion, it is evident that the activity of a lifetime might be confined to one or two deeds—that no progress could take place in development. A man might be occupied all day in dressing and undressing himself; the attitude of the body would absorb all his attention and energy; the washing of his hands or the fastening of a button would be as difficult to him on each occasion as to the child on its first trial; and he would, furthermore, be completely exhausted by his exertions. Think of the pains necessary to teach a child to stand, of the many efforts it must make and of the ease with which it at last stands unconscious of any effort. For while secondary automatic acts are accomplished with comparatively little weariness—in this regard approaching the organic movements or the original reflex movements—the conscious effort of the will soon produces exhaustion."

All psychologists recognize the effects of acquired habits of motion, thought, and even of feeling. They all agree in the fact that habits long indulged in and allowed to become "second nature" may become so firmly lodged in the subconscious mind that they require the strongest efforts of the will to dislodge them. Some even go so far as to say that such habits may successfully defy the will, and at first glance this may seem to be so, but The New Psychology shows that the subconsciousness may be trained so that the habits may be neutralized and eradicated, as we shall see a little later on. Kay believed that; "Habits and practices that have long been indulged in may set at defiance any power of the will that can be brought against them." But he was not aware that while they might defy the ordinary will, they might be fought on their own plane—the subconscious—and neutralized by the cultivation of new habits, with a comparatively small exertion of the will.

The philosophers and moralists have ever lamented the baneful power of undesirable habits, and have written and preached on the subject. Beecher said: "There is a wrong philosophy in supposing that a habit which has fixed itself in the fleshy nature can be overcome by the mere exertion of the will. It is not enough to resolve against it. You cannot vanquish it by the power of a resolution. To that must be added continuous training. " Archbishop Whately said: "Whatever a man may inwardly think and (with perfect sincerity say), you cannot fully depend upon his conduct till you know how he has been accustomed to act. For continued action is like a continued stream of water, which wears for itself a channel that it will not be easily turned from." St. Paul said: "I see another law in my members warring against the law of my mind...the good that I would I do not; but the evil that I would not, that I do....To will is present with me, but how to perform that which is good I know not." But it is useless to multiply quotations, or to fill pages explaining the power of habit, for good or evil. Everyone has had the actual experience of this action of the mind. What is needed is not so much to know that habit is, or what it is, as how to overcome and master it.

The New Psychology brushes aside the old technical explanations and theories regarding habit. It sees in habit the activities and phenomena of the subconsciousness, and therefore meets it on that plane. It realizes that all actions, ideas, or mental activities of any kind tend to pass from the control of the voluntary field of action on to the subconscious or involuntary plane. The mental path is a part of the subconscious mind and that region dominates the greater part of our mental life. Therefore instead of attacking the subconsciousness with the will—a long and heartbreaking task—we advise the neutralizing of the subconscious habit impressions by building up a new set of impressions directly opposed to the old ones that we wish to be rid of. In other words we kill out the old habits by building up new ones of an opposite nature. We fight the negative with the positive. We proceed to build new mental paths, and then travel over them as often as possible, so that in the end they become easier for the mind to travel over than the old ones, particularly if we avoid using the old ones as much as possible. The whole theory and practice may be summed up in these words: *Make new mental paths, and travel over them as often as possible.*

The following rules will be found useful in cultivating the new mental path, whether it be desired for its own sake, or else for the purpose of neutralizing an undesirable habit:

I. Form a mental picture in your imagination of the physical expressions of the desired habit. That is, try to see yourself as you will appear when the new habit is acquired. Imagine how you will look, talk and act. The firmer and clearer this mental image, the better will be the manifestation. The principle is that whatever is to be expressed in action, must first exist in the mind. So make the correct mental pattern. Cultivate this habit of seeing yourself as you wish to be—it sets a good example for your subconsciousness to follow.

II. Having formed the mental pattern of the physical expressions accompanying the desired habit, proceed to manifest these physical characteristics in your life. Act out the part you wish to play. Cultivate the physical characteristics of the character that you wish to make your own. There is a good psychological principle involved in all this—the principle that *physical expressions of a mental state tend to reproduce that mental state.* Just as it is true that thought takes form in action, so is it true that there is a reaction whereby the physical action

Mental Paths

reproduces the mental state which it represents. Endeavor to walk, talk, look and act like the character you wish to be yours. Do this gradually and you will soon be surprised to find that you are building yourself a new personality—without and within.

III. Endeavor to dwell in the desired mental state as much as possible—try to *feel* the desired mental state as often as possible. Cultivate the desired feeling, and travel over the new mental path as often as possible. You will find that this rule fits in well with the preceding one; for just as the outward expression induces the inner feeling, so does the inner feeling induce the outward action. And, so you see, one produces the other, and then the latter reproduces the first, and soon, until you have started an endless chain of cause and effect that will soon build your new mental path if you stick to it and do not allow yourself to be "sidetracked."

IV. Avoid the repetition of the undesirable habit with all your will, determination and individuality. While you are building up your new path try to keep your mind off the old one as much as possible. Do not indulge the old habit "just this once"—here is where you must make your fight. Avoid this "just this once" as you would a deadly viper—this is the danger point to be avoided. If you feel strongly tempted to repeat the old habit, here is your best chance to start in and perform an act along the lines of your new habit. This is much better than a straight will-fight, for it accomplishes more with less exertion and effort. Make it a point to perform the new habit just when the temptation confronts you—you will then wound the enemy in his most vital point, and just when he uncovers his weakest point to you. Like the shark and the Gila-monster, bad habits turn over on their backs to bite you, and in so doing they uncover their most vital point. Consequently this is the time and place for you to plunge in your spear of the new habit and wound the monster sorely. Every time you do this and defeat the enemy, the stronger do you become. Each time you overcome, you sap the energy from the enemy and turn it to good account. This is

The New Psychology

not mere "preaching"—it is the statement of a tried and proven truth of The New Psychology. Make it your own. Avoid above all the slipping back, once you have started. Some writers have said that this slipping back on the path of new habits, is like the dropping of a ball of yarn that you are winding up—in the drop you allow more to unwind than you can rewind in many turns of the wrist. But if you *should* happen to drop the ball, don't give up—pick it up and determinedly start to rewind it. But try hard to avoid the dropping—you *can* if you *will*.

Chapter X.

Thought And Character.

The old proverb, "As a man thinketh, so is he," has been pressed into active service of late, owing to the increase of interest in the various branches of The New Psychology under its many names and guises. The New Psychology is indeed the foundation principle of many different schools, cults, creeds and organizations, some of which would disown the relationship. It has passed as a truth, consequently, that a man's character, disposition, activities, and general personality are dependent in some mystic way with the character of his thoughts. Many interesting, unique and sometimes weird theories have been advanced to account for this fact, but to students of The New Psychology the phenomenon is seen to rest upon a purely scientific basis, in no way connected with mysticism or strange dogmas.

The working out of the "As a man thinketh" idea is simply a matter of applied idealism, and applied idealism is closely connected with the phenomena of the subconscious region of mentality. A man is not so much the result of what he "thinks" as of what he "feels." Character building depends far more upon the feeling and emotional side of one's nature than upon the purely intellectual and rational process of the mind. A man may "think" continually upon mathematics or some other abstract subject, but he does not become a mathematical problem or an abstract entity. These thoughts have an effect upon his character only so far as they serve to inhibit or neutralize his capacity for feeling or manifesting emotion—as pure thought they have no formative power. But select any man who is interested in anything that arouses his desires, feelings, emotions, or any other mental faculties having a close relationship to the subconscious region of his mind, and you will find him molding a character in accordance with those desires, feelings, or emotions. It is all a matter of supplying the subconscious mentality with a certain kind of impressions.

It is frequently said, and truly, that a man grows to resemble his ideals. But this only supports the contention we have just made. A man's ideals are the things he loves—the opposites of the things he hates. And both love and hate are matters belonging to the emotional and feeling side of his mentality, not to the intellectual side. His ideals are bound up with his feelings, emotions, desires. He may not be able to explain them intellectually, particularly if he has not acquired, the art of using his intellectual faculties. Persons of very small intellectual power have strong tendencies, desires, and ideals, as well as their brothers who have developed the intellect. Even the man who finds a keen pleasure in exercising his intellect—who feels the joy of pure reason—finds the "feeling" or desire the motive power. The intellect is a cold thing—a machine that performs the work set for it by one's desires or necessities, the latter manifesting as feelings. And so, at the last, it will be seen that a man's ideals depend upon his likes and dislikes—feelings and emotions.

And the ideal held by one imparts interest in all that concerns or relates to it; and interest is the strong motive of attention; and attention is the phonographic needle of the mind that makes the impressions upon the subconscious records. And so, you see, one's ideals serve to set into activity the chain of cause and effect that results in storing away in his mind numerous clear and deep impressions that manifest a marked effect upon his character. By the constant use of these impressions he builds the mental paths over which he travels often. And the oftener he travels these mental paths, the more "set" does his character become. And so in the end we may see the truth of that axiom of The New Psychology: *A man grows to resemble the thing he loves*. Tell us what a man loves, and we will tell you what the man is. And so: As a Man *Loveth*, so is he.

Another axiom of The New Psychology—two axioms in fact—twin axioms—here they are: (1) Feelings manifest in action; (2) A man follows the line of his Strongest Interest. These two axioms work together. It is one of the fundamental ideas of The New Psychology that mental states, particularly the states of desires, feelings, and emotions, manifest themselves in outward activity. This fact is brought out in every branch of the teachings. Prof. William James lays great stress upon this truth of psychology. He says: "All consciousness is motor;" and, "We might say that every possible feeling produces a movement, and that the movement is a movement of the entire organism, and of each and all its parts." The same authority goes still further when he says: "I now proceed to urge the vital point of my whole theory, which is this: If we fancy some strong emotion, and then try to abstract from our consciousness of it all the feelings of its bodily symptoms, we find that we have nothing left behind." In other words, that there is always a physical and outward manifestation arising from an inward mental state. This being so, we can readily see why our actions tend to fall into the mold or pattern created by our feelings.

We are constantly acting, usually unconsciously, in accordance with our predominant desires, likes, or dislikes, which arise from feelings. It is only when we are forced to make a new decision that the matter rises to the field of consciousness, and even then we are influenced by our feelings, tempered by our judgment. Our physical lives are regulated by our mental states, and our mental states are largely what we make them. And so we might add: As a man Feels so Does he. And, when we realize that our feelings depend largely upon our control, or lack of control, of the material taken into our subconscious mentality, then do we begin to see why The New Psychology lays so much stress upon the Mastery of the Subconscious. The materials of our feelings are all taken from our subconscious storehouse, and what we put in there comes out in the shape of feelings and emotions, and these in turn take form in action. And so each day we act in accordance with what we have placed in our subconsciousness or else have allowed others to place in there for us.

The second of these two axioms is: A man follows the lines of his strongest Interest. This should awaken every individual to a realization of the importance of beginning the practice of placing his Ego on the throne of his mentality and choosing intelligently the objects of his interest. The majority of persons follow the line of the least resistance in this respect, and allow themselves to become interested in many things regardless of the importance of those things to their well-being. To many persons the suggestion that they have the *power* to select the objects of their interest seems absurd, and provocative of laughter. They are so accustomed to regard interest, feelings, desires and emotions as things beyond their control, that they make no attempt to exercise a voluntary control over them. It is true that these mental states do not spring from pure intellectual effort—that they spring from the depths of the subconscious mentality unbidden, in most cases. But the proven facts of The New Psychology show us plainly that the Ego may assume control of these involuntary mental states, and either encourage and develop them, or else restrain or inhibit them entirely. Just as the will may assume control of certain involuntary muscles of the body, so may the Ego assume control of its entire mental kingdom and mold, and build, change and improve every department of its mental workshop. By concentration and attention, interest may be directed to and held upon certain things, and removed and kept away from other things. Interest kindles desire, and lack of interest causes desire to die. And interest results from attention, and may be controlled by the will. And the will is the chief instrument of the Ego. By using the reasoning and judicial faculties of the mind in the matter of right selection of objects of interest, the positive qualities and objects may be selected in preference to the negative ones. And this being done, we are well started on our way toward character building, mastery and power.

Interest in a subject or object which at first seems to be interesting, may be acquired and developed by selecting the most attractive or least repulsive detail, item, or part of the thing, ignoring for the time being the other parts, and acquainting oneself thoroughly with its features, characteristics, and qualities. If one will but use the will in the matter of focusing the attention upon an uninteresting object or subject for a time, there will arise features or aspects of interest which in turn will lead to others; then other parts of the same thing may be taken up in the same way, and so on. Lack of interest in a thing, as a rule, arises from either lack of acquaintance with the inwardness of the thing, or else from over attention to it, which has produced weariness and desire for change. In the first case, the remedy is a better acquaintance; in the second, a restful change of attention to something else, after which a new interest will spring up.

If one wishes to destroy, restrain, or inhibit an undue interest in a subject or object that is considered not conducive to the well-being of the individual, the rule of The New Psychology is to concentrate the attention and interest upon a subject or object diametrically opposed to the first one. It will be found that the new interest will inhibit or neutralize the old one, and this process is much easier than that of forcibly killing out the old interest by use of the will. *Concentrate on the opposite*, is the rule of The New Psychology when one wishes to restrain, inhibit, or destroy a mental condition in oneself.

Above all, do not make the mistake of regarding your feelings, emotions or interest as You. Remember always that You—the Real You—are the "I"—the Ego—the Master of all mental states and conditions, whose weapon and trusty instrument is the will.

Chapter XI.

Emotion.

It is very difficult to define Emotion, and yet everyone recognizes just what is meant by the term. Emotion is the term employed to denote the set of mental activities belonging to the "feeling" side of mentation, as distinguished from sensation, thought or volition. There is but little difference between what we call "feeling," as used in this sense, and what we call "emotion." The difference is largely one of degree. Feeling is the simple form of emotion; or emotion the more complex form of feeling. You, of course, realize that we are speaking of the mental state known as "feeling," and not of physical sensation. A sensation is the result of some internal or external physical substance registering its impressions upon our mentality. A "feeling" is a mental state producing an experience of pleasure or pain, in some degree or combination. An emotion is a mental state composed of a number of feelings, or the average of a number of feelings—a complex state of feeling. Feeling or emotion may arise from the contemplation or consciousness of some object outside of one's self, or from the memory of some occurrence, or from imagination in which some thing or occurrence is pictured to the mind. It is not a matter of reason or will—it belongs to the subconscious region of mentation.

The New Psychology

Like all other subconscious mentation Emotion has its relation to something in the past—something that has been put into the subconscious region of the mind. These past impressions may have been recorded in the subconscious mentality during the life of the individual, in which case its recurrence and emergence into the field of consciousness is caused by an involuntary call upon the memory. Or the past impression may be one of those remarkable race-memories coming to us down the passage of time according to the law of heredity, and recalled involuntarily. In either case the result is the same—an emergence from the subconscious region of some impression or series of impressions from the past, arousing in us strange feelings and mental excitement. Pain and pleasure are elemental feelings, and certain objects producing them throughout the ages have left upon us the subconscious impressions which result in the feelings and emotions inspired by those things.

There is a close connection between Emotion and physical expression—these two act and react upon each other. We are pleased, and our mouth takes an upward turn, and queer little wrinkles form around the eyes—we smile. We are sad, and our mouth droops downward, and our entire countenance, and our general attitude as well, denote the quality of the emotion. Anger, fear, jealousy, curiosity, and all the other emotions register themselves in outward expression. Actors and experimental psychologists know that if one will imitate the outward physical expressions of any emotion, earnestly and persistently, there will come about a reaction that will result in the production of that particular mental state, or emotion. Smile earnestly, and persistently, and you will feel cheerful. Frown and clench the fists, and you will soon feel cross and angry. In this fact of emotional action and reaction there rests a whole field of Self Mastery and Self Control. Those who will accept this hint have a valuable weapon of character—building and mental-control at their disposal.

Emotion

People are largely what their emotions have made them. But this, while true, is only a half-truth. It is true that unrestrained emotion adds repeated impressions upon the subconscious mentality, and deepens the original impressions at each repetition, until finally the character is so influenced by these customary phases of emotion that it becomes "set" as does a mold that has hardened. But The New Psychology also gives the other half of the truth. While recognizing that a man's character is largely determined by the character of the emotions in which he has indulged, it also holds firmly to the correlated fact that a man's emotions may be mastered, regulated, changed, developed, encouraged, discouraged, or inhibited altogether, by the exercise of the power of the Master of the Mind—the Ego. From a state of slavery to his "feelings" and emotions, one may rise to a state of mastery. Instead of allowing the feelings and emotional side of one's self to run away with one, the individual may press his emotions into service and use them to his advantage and well-being. The uncontrolled emotions are like a number of horses running away with the stage-coach, the driver sitting helpless upon his seat and not dreaming of exerting his controlling power. But the driver—the Ego—once awakened to a sense of his power, may draw in the reins and by exerting his skill and strength soon have the horses under control and doing good work in pulling along the coach. That the emotions may be controlled to a certain degree, every person knows in a way. But the majority do not dream of the extent of the control, nor are they aware that emotions may be developed and cultivated. When the Ego comes to his own, all these things are possible.

It is impossible in the brief space to be devoted to this one phase of the subject to give detailed instruction regarding the cultivation and control of the emotions. But, nevertheless, we intend giving you the general principles underlying the same, that you may apply them to suit the requirements of your particular case, adapting them intelligently to your own requirements. In the same way you may be enabled to direct the emotional development of those around you who will listen to your advice and accept your guidance.

I. In the first place, remember that emotions are subject to the rule of Habit. By reading the chapter of this book devoted to Mental Paths, you may see that habit-emotions may be mastered, developed or restrained. The fundamental law of habit is repetition—repetition deepens the habit impression and infuses new life into the particular idea, thought or emotion governed by it. Therefore if you wish to cultivate an emotion, repeat it by careful and constant practice and exercise until it becomes habitual. If you would restrain or inhibit an emotion, refuse to allow it to manifest as much as possible; confine it to as little outward expression as possible when it does manifest; prevent the corresponding physical expression as much as possible; *and above all cultivate the emotion exactly opposite to the one you wish to restrain.* This is a general rule in restricting or inhibiting all mental states—cultivate their opposites. This is according to the law of opposites which is operative in the mental realm as well as in the physical—to counteract cold, apply heat; to counteract heat, apply cold. This is the Law of Neutralization.

II. Observe the Law of Physical Expression. That is, remember that if you indulge the physical expression of an emotion you tend to produce the emotion itself. And contrarily, if you restrain the physical expression of an emotion you tend to inhibit the emotion itself. This is a valuable rule of The New Psychology. This truth has perhaps never been so well, and authoritatively stated as by Prof. Wm. James, when he said: "Refuse to express a passion, and it dies. Count ten before venting your anger, and its occasion seems ridiculous. Whistling to keep up courage is no mere figure of speech. On the other hand, sit all day in a moping posture, sigh, and reply to everything with a dismal voice, and your melancholy lingers....If we wish to conquer undesirable emotional tendencies in ourselves, we must assiduously, and

Emotion

in the first instance cold-bloodedly, go through the outward movements of those contrary dispositions which we prefer to cultivate....Smooth the brow, brighten the eye, contract the dorsal rather than the ventral aspect of the frame, and speak in a major key, pass the genial compliment, and your heart must be frigid indeed if it does not gradually thaw."

III. Use the Imagination in the direction of reproducing the emotions we desire to cultivate, or else the opposites of those we wish to restrain. Impressions by the imagination are similar to those made as the result of outside stimulus. Go over the desirable emotion in your imagination often, forming a mental picture of outward circumstances calculated to arouse the desired feeling, or the feeling opposed to the undesired one. In your leisure hours practice this method, making your pictures as vivid as possible, and filling in as many details as you can. With each repetition you will strengthen the impression upon the records of your subconscious mentality, and tend to establish the habit of emotion that you desire. Put attention and interest into the work, of course, and you will soon grow to enjoy these day-dream exercises. To those who do not understand the creative effect of the imagination, all this may appear silly and a waste of time. But when one realizes that the imagination is not mere fancy, but an active, potent faculty of the mind in its creative work, it will be seen that this exercise of the imagination is in the direction of building emotional paths over which the mind will soon grow accustomed to tread.

IV. And, in this, as in everything else, do not lose sight of the employment of the Will—that mighty instrument of the Ego, wherewith all the other faculties may be shaped and developed, or restrained. We do not mean that it is necessary to make violent use of the will in this work, for that is neither necessary nor advisable. But hold the will firmly to the task when occasion presents itself, particularly when the work to be done is in the nature of restraining an emotion. Use the will to say "No!" to it. The use of the will in the direction of self-mastery and self-restraint is one of its noblest uses. To the Ego the will is the most valuable instrument of government, and when rightly used it has an almost miraculous power, particularly in the direction of restraint. It is the reins by which the Ego holds in its fiery steeds, and guides them aright and safely.

If you will but heed these four rules, and employ them intelligently and faithfully, you will have taken a mighty step in Self-Mastery. This is another lesson of The New Psychology.

Chapter XII.

Imagination.

THE NEW Psychology regards the faculty of Imagination, in its creative aspect with a degree of consideration foreign to the older view. The latter regarded the imagination in its negative phase of "fancy" and idle dreaming rather than in its positive phase of creative activity. While it is true that the imagination is more frequently employed by the average person in its negative phase than in its positive phase—in its aspect of fanciful, unreal imaging rather than in its aspect of "seeing ahead,' planning, creating and forecasting—this does not lessen the importance of the faculty, the fault being with the persons so using it. It has been quite the fashion among so-called "practical" people to speak slightingly of the faculty of the imagination as representing all that was impractical, unreal, fanciful, having no basis in actuality—imagination was confounded with "imaginary." These people overlooked or ignored the fact that all inventive and creative work of the mind is performed by this faculty. The use of the terms "imaginative," "imaginary," etc., shows how firmly fixed in the public mind is this half-view of the wonderful faculty of the Imagination—one of the most important in the mind of man. It is one of the distinctive features of The New Psychology that it gives to

The New Psychology

Imagination its proper place in the list of the positive faculties of the mind, and urges the scientific control and development of the faculty.

The misconception regarding the imagination arises from the fact that it is most commonly seen in its negative phase—involuntary imagination, or "day dreaming." This involuntary use of the imagination, without purpose or control, amounts to but little more than idle dreaming, and the term "day dreaming" is well applied to it. In this use of the faculty—"misuse" would be the better term—the subconscious is allowed to unfold into the field of consciousness some of its wonderful stores, following a first thought along the lines of association, and allowing an idle grouping of mental images, without design or intelligent order, and above all *without purpose or use*. This is mere dreaming, and is a habit which obtains quite a hold over people if indulged in, and is very apt to lead them away from the actual activities of life. It is a mild form of mental intoxication, the effects of which are often as disastrous as those of other forms of intoxication. This idle dreaming tends to weaken the will, and render infirm the purposive faculties of the mind. The most harmful result of this practice is that it usurps the place rightfully belonging to action. It is so much easier and so much more pleasant to dream of accomplishments, than to attempt to make them come true in actual life. The habitual daydreamer gradually loses the desire to participate in the activities of life, and slowly sinks into a mere passive existence, doing as little actual work as possible, and always longing for his hours of dream-life as the morphine victim longs for his drug or the liquor victim longs for his glass.

Prof. Halleck has well said of the above tendency: "The day-dreamer attains eminence at one bound. He is without trouble a victorious general on a vast battlefield, an orator swaying thousands, a millionaire with every amusement at his command, a learned man confounding the wisest, a president, an emperor, a czar. After reveling in these imaginative sweets, the dry bread of actual toil becomes exceedingly distasteful. It is so much easier to live in regions where everything comes at the stroke of the magic-wand of fancy." And recognizing this fact, The New Psychology sets its face squarely against this negative form of the use of the imagination, and teaches that it may be overcome by transmuting the energies of the dream into images of things connected with the life work of the individual, character building, self-mastery, and general actual creative work—the positive phase of imagination, in fact.

The New Psychology holds that the positive use of the Imagination along creative or constructive lines is worthy of cultivation and development by scientific methods, for the reason that by its intelligent and purposive application it leads to all progress and advancement, attainment and realization. Creative and constructive imagination furnishes the pattern, design or mold of the future action or material manifestation. The imagination is the architect of deeds, actions, and accomplishments. A well-known woman of this land once made the remark that she prayed that her sons might be given the active power of creative and constructive imagination—and her wish was a wise one, for from that power are derived the plans of future accomplishment.

Sir Benjamin Brodie once said: "Physical investigation, more than anything besides, helps to teach us the actual value and right use of the imagination—of that wondrous faculty, which, when left to ramble uncontrolled, leads us astray in a wilderness of perplexities and errors, a land of mists and shadows; but which, properly controlled by experience and reflection, becomes the noblest attribute of man, the source of poetic genius, the instrument of discovery in science, without the aid of which Newton would never have invented fluxions nor Davy have decomposed the earths and alkalies, nor would Columbus have found another continent." Tyndall, the great English scientist of the last century, said: "We are gifted with the power of imagination, and by this power we can lighten the darkness which surrounds the world of the senses. There are tories, even in science, who regard imagination as a faculty to be feared and avoided rather than employed. They have observed its action in weak vessels, and are unduly impressed by its disasters. But they might with equal truth point to exploded boilers as an argument against the use of steam. Bounded and conditioned by co-operant reason, imagination becomes the mightiest instrument of the physical discoverer. Newton's passage from a falling apple to a falling moon was, at the outset, a leap of the imagination."

In short in considering the theory of the creative and constructive work of the imagination, it may be said that it is but another example of that fundamental and basic principle of The New Psychology—the principle of the Ego using its instruments instead of allowing them to use it. The Ego uses its imaginative faculty along creative and constructive lines, instead of allowing the faculty to run away with it in the direction of idle dreaming and fanciful imagining. It is the Positive use of the mind, instead of the Negative. This principle runs through the entire field of The New Psychology, and this is but another instance of its application.

And now arises the question: How may the Imagination be cultivated and directed along creative and constructive lines of activity! The New Psychology answers this in numerous ways. Let us take a hasty glance at these answers.

I. In the first place the imagination, or rather the subconscious region of the mind, to which the imagination belongs, should be filled with a variety of well selected images—selected with the idea of profitable use. The attention should be directed toward, and held upon subjects and objects calculated to be useful and profitable to the mind. For from this stock of mental images, stored in the subconscious region, the finished product of the imagination must be formed. And the images should be clear and definite, and well impressed.

Imagination

II. Cultivate the creative and constructive use of the imagination. That is, acquire the habit of using the imagination in the direction of "laying out" and planning actual work ahead of you. Get into the way of making definite plans of work and action, and then following out these plans in action. Get into the way of "planning" things, even little things, instead of merely allowing them to "happen." In other words, get into the way of seeing the thing in "your mind's eye" before you manifest it physically. Try to improve upon present methods, and to advance along the lines of your occupation—not necessarily making changes just for the sake of change, but try to *improve*, if even but a little, in the accomplishment of the things you do. There is always room for improvement and so use your imagination in this way. You will find that, after the habit is acquired, you will experience considerable pleasure in materializing your mental images—in accomplishing the things you have seen in your mind's eye.

III. Avoid as a pestilence the negative habit of idle "day-dreaming," for the reasons given a little farther back. Let your day dreams be purposive, and always with the idea of making them come true. Keep the idea of "planning" in your mind, as an antidote for the tendency to idly dream.

IV. In your use of the imagination, in the direction above indicated, always hold to the central purpose of the thought or image. Build up, and tear down, alter and change the image, as much as you see fit, but always with the idea of improving and completing the original idea. Keep to the main idea, and do not allow yourself to be side-tracked.

V. Learn to discard mental images that do not fit in with your plan. A little practice will enable you to brush aside images that do not fit into the plan, instead of allowing them to "float in" as is the case with ordinary day dreaming.

VI. Subject all your mental images to the test: Will they make me stronger, better and more powerful?—are they Positive or Negative? Reject the Negatives and hold fast to the Positives.

VII. Use the imagination in the direction of *seeing yourself as you wish to be*. And cultivate the habit of forming a clear mental picture of things and conditions as you wish them to be. By familiarizing your mind with the conditions you want, you form the proper mental paths to lead to the realization. The imagination is your pattern-maker, die-sinker, mold-maker—make it do its work properly, for as is the pattern, die, or mold, so will be the materialization.

Chapter XIII.

Memory.

One of the most wonderful faculties of the mind, and one of the most useful, is that which we call memory. Strictly speaking, memory can scarcely be called a faculty of the mind—it is one of the mind's powers. The importance of memory may be realized when one considers that the entire education of the individual depends upon memory for its virtue and efficacy. Without memory, experience would teach the mind nothing, and each act would be new every time it was performed, each object new every time it was seen; in short, the mind of man would always remain as the mind of the very young child, and advancement would be impossible. There is a close relationship between the memory of the individual, and the inherited instincts of the race, the latter being but manifestations of race-memory analogous to the dimly remembered experiences of days past.

Psychologists do not attempt to define memory—it remains a mystery. But The New Psychology teaches that it is a function of the subconscious region of the mind. As we have seen, the subconscious region is a great store-house in which are stored all sorts of mental impressions in great variety. These impressions may be re-presented to the field of consciousness upon occasions. There is very little difference between the presentation to the field of consciousness of the worked-up material of subconscious thought, inherited instinct, acquired habit impulses, etc., on the one hand, and recorded memory impressions on the other. These manifestations bear a striking resemblance to each other, and are readily recognized as belonging to the same family.

The work of the subconscious region, so far as the activities of memory are concerned, seems to consist in the presentation of plastic mind-stuff to receive thereon the impressions of the senses, the imagination, and of ideas evolved by thought. We may best understand the workings of this region of the mind if we will but indulge in the fanciful idea of tiny mental workers in charge of the memory records. Of course there are no such entities, but the memory works as if there were, and we may understand its workings by indulging in this fanciful style of presentation of the facts.

In the first place, let us imagine these tiny workers as having on hand an unfailing supply of tiny plastic records upon which to receive the impressions passed on by the report of our senses, our imagination, and our ideas. Each sensation, thought, or idea makes an impression on one of these records, varying in depth and clearness according to the degree of attention bestowed upon it. If the sensation, thought, or idea is repeated, the same record receives it and the impression is deepened. The impression may also be deepened by having the workers bring the record into the field of consciousness, and then allowing the imagination to make repeated impressions upon it. But this last practice sometimes works in an unexpected manner, for the imagination may indulge itself in enlarging, and extending the original impression and changing its character, and if this be done several times the record will be changed and it will be almost impossible to distinguish the original impression from those added by the imagination. Common experience will show us the truth of this last statement, for who does not know of cases where people have added to a true tale repeatedly told, until at last it becomes entirely different from the original facts, and yet the teller of the tale imagines that he is telling the exact truth.

But these little workers have many other tasks besides that of taking the impressions. They realize that they are continually being called upon to furnish the Ego with these records in order that it may avail itself of its stored away facts. In order to do this they must have a perfect system of storing and indexing the records, with countless cross-indexes, cross-references, etc. They must arrange each recorded thought, sensation, or idea so that it may be associated with others of its kind, so that when a record is examined it may bring with it its associations in time, space, and kind, that the Ego may be able to think continuously, intelligently, and orderly. What would be the use of remembering a single fact, or idea, if the associated ideas or facts were not to be had? Intelligent thought would be impossible under such circumstances. So important is this law of association in memory, that the entire value of the memory depends upon it. Teachers of Memory Culture lay great stress upon this fact. They teach their students that in cases where they are unable to recall a desired fact or idea, the next best thing is to think of some associated fact, scene, or idea, and lo! once having laid hold of a link in the chain, it is merely a matter of time before the missing record is found. It is like a great system of cross-indexing. If you cannot remember a thing, find something associated with it, and then run down the index, and you will find what you want.

But, you may say, how do you account for the apparent difference in the relative powers of memory displayed by different individuals? Very easily. The relative powers of the memory in different individuals depend largely upon two factors: (1) the quality and degree of attention; and (2) upon the training, by intelligent practice, of the subconscious faculties having to do with memory—the tiny "workers," in fact. You will see by reference to the preceding chapter on Attention that the degree of mental impression depends largely upon that faculty. Attention regulates the degree of depth and clearness of the impression upon the records of the memory. The persons who manifest a knowledge of any particular line undoubtedly have given much attention to the matters connected with that line, devoting interest and concentration to the task. Upon other lines, possessing little or no interest to them, they have bestowed but little attention, and the result is that their records are shallow and imperfect. The records, like that of a phonograph, merely bear the impressions placed upon them, and are true in quality and degree to the original—Attention is the phonographic needle of the memory. The teacher of Memory Culture must first teach the cultivation of Attention, for otherwise the memory teaching will be of no avail, for unless the original impressions be clear the reproduction cannot be clear.

But, even among persons of equal powers of Attention, there will be manifested different degrees of power of recollection or memory, even where the same degree of interest is had. This is due to the degree of efficiency of the faculties of the memory, which we are fancifully considering under the guise of the tiny workers of the subconscious region. No matter how anxious and willing to serve these little workers may be—no matter how efficient they may be naturally—still *they need to be drilled*. Like any other army they must be drilled, and put through their motions in order to acquire a high degree of proficiency. And they must be kept in practice in order to retain their efficiency. Just imagine that you had under your supervision a corps of millions of tiny filing clerks, porters, registers, and what not, who had the charge and care of millions of valuable records, their duties requiring a high degree of proficiency and efficiency. Would you expect the best results from them without drill, practice and exercise in their duties? Do you not know that every army, office force, or other body of individuals gets "rusty" from lack of practice? Constant practice, and demand of the best work brings a corps of workers up to a fine edge of proficiency and efficiency, and creates interest in the work before them. And it is so with the little workers of the mind. And it is a well established fact of The New Psychology that intelligent training and exercise will develop a high degree of efficiency and service in this corps of workers of the subconscious region of the mind.

There have been many systems of Memory Culture devised by many teachers, for some of which high prices have been charged. But the majority of these systems are artificial in their nature, and depend upon complicated systems of association for their results. Many have merit, but the only natural system is that favored by The New Psychology, which is based upon the actual working principles of the subconscious mentality itself. In this system there is instruction given, first, in the receiving of impressions by means of Attention and Interest, along scientific lines, and by methods which experience has taught to be practicable and efficacious; and second, by an intelligent application of the principles of natural association and "recording" of impressions. There is no special secret or mystery about this system—it is not a "patent" system owned by any one. It is merely a systematic, scientific arrangements of the ascertained psychological principles of memory, coupled with advice, instruction and training along the lines of tried methods.

The cultivation of the memory is really a cultivation of the entire mind, for a moment's thought will show you that the whole process of intelligent thought depends upon memory as a foundation. Without memory the possessor of even the finest brain would be little more than an imbecile. Moreover, the cultivation of the memory naturally sharpens the powers of perception, and increases the use of the will. In fact, in any system of natural memory training the entire mental faculties receive practice and development. It would be impossible to train the memory naturally without bringing into play the perceptive faculties, and the sense of orderly mentation. And when this is considered and recognized, does it not seem almost a crime against the race that our schools pay no attention whatsoever, in the great majority of cases, to the training and cultivation of this important faculty of the mind? Ordinary intelligence would dictate that the child should be trained in rational memory exercises, even from the first grade. This is one of the results that The New Psychology hopes to achieve.

The second book of "The New Psychology Series" will be devoted to Memory Development. Those specially interested in this subject are referred to the said work for detailed instructions.

Chapter XIV.

Desire.

Desire is the great motive power of life—the great incentive to action. A man is largely what the quality and degree of his desires have led him to be. Desire is the fire which produces the steam of action. No matter how splendidly a man may be equipped with the other mental faculties—no matter how great may be his powers of perception, reason, judgment, application, or even will—unless he also possesses a strong desire for accomplishment the other faculties will never be brought into action. Desire is the great inciter of mental and physical activities—the arouser of the will. As we have said in writing on the subject, "Desire is at the bottom of all feeling. Before we can love or hate, there must be desire. Before we can have ambition or aspiration there must be desire. Before we can manifest courage and energy there must be desire. Desire for something must underlie all life-action, desire conscious or subconscious. Abstract thought is a cold bare thing, lacking vitality and warmth—desire is filled with life, throbbing, longing, wanting, craving, insisting, and ever pressing outward toward action. Desire is indeed the phase of mental action that is the motive-force." We may call desire by the more popular terms,

The New Psychology

"ambition," "aspiration," "longing for attainment," etc., but desire is ever the basic principle of all longing, wishing, wanting.

Not only is our life largely determined by the nature and quality of our desires, but our accomplishments and attainments depend very materially upon the *degree* of our desires. The quality of desire determines in what mental path we shall travel, but the degree determines how far we shall travel. The majority of people manifest but little desire—they want many things, it is true, but they do not want them "hard enough." Their desires end in mere wishing, and wanting—they do not reach the stage of action. Desire unexpressed is like steam in a boiler that has not reached the intensity required to drive the engine. Increase the intensity and degree, and the steam rushes out and in a moment the pistons are moving and the wheels revolving. The great men in all walks of life have possessed strong desires for attainment, accomplishment, possession—the principle being the same in all these cases. Their desire was of such a degree that it reached the explosive point, and manifested in action. It is generally taught that Will is the great motive power of the mind. This is not correct, unless it is assumed that Will is the active phase of desire. Desire is the motive power that imparts the energy to the action. The will is more as a guiding, directing force which applies the energy of the desire. Will is cold, and steely—desire is glowing with heat and fire. The will may, and does, guide, direct, restrict, hold back and even destroy the desire in some cases—nevertheless, desire supplies the energy for action. No matter how strong a will the individual may have, unless he has strong desire to use the will he does not use it. No matter how clearly a man may see how a thing may be done, no matter how well his reason and judgment may point out the way, no matter how clear an imagination he may possess to picture the plan of the action—unless he be possessed of the desire to act, and that in a goodly degree, then there will be no action.

Desire

And yet it must be admitted that the will is the highest instrument of the Ego, for by it the individual is enabled to create desires within himself; or else change existing desires; or else kill existing desires in his subconscious mentality. All this is possible, but still, before he can do any of these things he must first *desire* to do them so that even in this final analysis desire is seen to supply the motive force and to be the incentive to action.

The individual who allows desire to master him is to be pitied. And yet this is true of the great majority of the race, who are swayed this way and that way by their desires, and who have not acquired the art of submitting their desires to the judgment of their reason and the control of their will. The man who has acquired the art of controlling and directing his desires has traveled far on the road to attainment. For to such a man desire becomes a faithful and efficient servant, inspiring action and interest, and therefore all the other mental faculties.

It seems strange at first thought to think of the Ego deliberately using the judgment and will to incite desire in the subconscious mind in order to inspire the mind to action and attainment. But when it is remembered that this is merely another instance of the Ego using its tools and instruments in its own workshop in order to turn out the finished product of action, the matter seems plainer. The Ego without the mental workshop would be simply the "pure Ego" devoid of its machinery of expression and manifestation. As some of the Hindu philosophers have expressed it, the Ego would be like a man who could see but who had no legs, and who could not move by himself. This legless man (the Ego) meets another man (the mental faculties) who is blind, but who possesses a good pair of legs. The legless man mounts on the shoulders of the blind man, and the two start off on their travels, the upper man directing and controlling the man with the legs. If the man with the legs were allowed to run away or to refuse obedience, the pair would come to grief—and yet without him the pair could not progress. Each performs his part—and each needs the other—but the man who can see must always be the master and director. The Ego must always control and master the mental faculties, else they will rob it of its power.

To the average person who thinks at all about it, the matter of the origin of desires is veiled in mystery. He knows that he does not evolve them from his reason, for they seem to spring into consciousness from nowhere. And yet the psychologist knows that all mental states have their preceding causes and reason. There is but one answer to the riddle—*all desires emerge from the subconscious region*, either in the sense of being a reproduction of some emotion or feeling previously experienced and brought into the field of consciousness as a memory, or else in the sense of being a response of the stored up impressions brought into new activity in response to the appearance of some outside thing which awakens the latent forces. In either case desire emerges from the subconsciousness and is distinctly a phenomenon of that region of the mind. And accordingly, the methods for cultivating or restricting the subconscious mental states are applicable in the case of desires.

Desire is connected on one side with the feeling and emotional phase of mentation, and on the other with the phase of volition or will. On its inner side desire is but the product of various states and combinations of states of feeling and emotion. On this side it is connected with the mental life of the past—either racial or individual. On its outer side it is connected with volition or will, and relates to the present or future. A desire must always have as its basis some antecedent feeling or emotion, and at the same time some antecedent experience, either racial or individual. One never desires a thing unless he has some subconscious experience of feeling. And moreover this experience presupposes some antecedent knowledge of the thing desired. One never desires a thing unless there is registered in his subconsciousness a trace of knowledge of the thing itself. Show a person an object of which he has no

Desire

registration of previous experience, racial or individual, and he feels no desire or repulsion for the thing—for he knows nothing of its qualities. Let him undergo an experience regarding it, and ever after he will have a definite feeling for or against it, subject of course to revision on account of further knowledge. In this connection it must be remembered that repulsion, aversion, dislike or fear are but negative forms of desire—are in fact desires "not to" experience the thing. And consequently the same laws and rules are applicable to aversion, repulsion or fear, as well as to the phases of positive desire. It naturally follows that if the Ego exerts a control over its subconscious region of mentality it may develop or restrain the desires emerging therefrom. By holding the attention on one set of ideas or objects in the imagination, by means of the will, one may "grow" the desires he thinks conducive to his well-being, and likewise may restrain or inhibit those calculated to work against his well-being. Desires grow by the amount of attention and interest bestowed upon them, and wither and decay in proportion that the attention and interest are withheld from them.

In order to cultivate a set of desires, one should resolutely determine to devote to them much attention and interest. That is, he should think of objects calculated to encourage and nourish those particular desires; make frequent mental images of them in the imagination; devote much interest and thought to all connected with them. In short, keep the objects calculated to bring forth the desire in mind as much as possible. In the same way desires which one thinks well to restrain, destroy or inhibit, should be treated in two ways: (1) by resolutely keeping the attention and interest away from them, for by so doing you shut off the nourishment from them and they wither and die by reason thereof; and (2) by keeping well in mind the thoughts and feelings calculated to grow, nourish and foster the desires of the direct opposite of the dying desires—by so doing you let in the sunshine that drives out the darkness. This is the antidote to the bane of unworthy desires—kill them out by encouraging their opposites. The New Psychology holds that the Ego has full power to regulate its own desires—to encourage or restrain them as it will—by the power of attention and interest under the control of the reason and will. This plan requires perseverance—but so does everything else worth having. Let your Ego be the Master, and insist that desire be the servant and not the ruler of your self.

Chapter XV.

The Will.

As we said in the last chapter, desire is connected with the will. One may desire much and often without exerting the will into action. But it is difficult to conceive of the will acting without desire, consciously or subconsciously exerted. One may want to do a thing, and yet not do it; but it is almost impossible to conceive of one willing to do a thing unless under the motive of desire, either in the sense of want on the one side, or fear, repulsion or aversion on the other. And so, at the last, will is seen to be the active expression of desire in some form. But this does not mean that one must act upon every desire, or that one does so. The experience of everyone informs him that desire may be restrained, restricted or completely inhibited, and that the will instead of responding to the urge of the desire may refuse to do so, and may even act to restrain the desire and drive it from the mind.

And so we approach the consideration of the will in, its threefold aspect. On the one side will is seen to blend into desire—so closely that it is difficult to distinguish the dividing line. Some hold that desire is but one of the phases of the will. The second phase of will is seen in the manifestation of that which we call "choice"—the ability to select and choose between objects of desire. In fact, to many this is considered the principal function of the will. The dictionaries give as one of the fundamental meanings of will: "The act of determining; deciding; making choice, etc." Now this "making choice" is a complex matter, involving the weighing of conflicting desires, weighing them by the light of the reason, striking an average, and finally determining upon the choice. But this choice is determined largely by reason of the "habit paths" of the mind, for the reason that it is always the line of least resistance to repeat an accustomed object in preference to a new and unaccustomed one. So after all the subconscious plays a most important part in the choice, not only by reason of the relative strength of the several desires presented to the will, but also by reason of the "mental paths" of the mind. The average person is governed almost altogether by the feelings and emotions in making choices of this kind—in using the will in this way. Only those who have attained some degree of mental control are able to subject these conflicting desires to the bright light of the reason, and to determine accordingly. To do this requires the ability to detach the Ego, in a measure, from the subconscious influences and to allow it to dwell on the judicial bench of the reason and to weigh and decide impartially according to the merits of the case. The man or woman who has attained this stage is well on the way toward mental mastery. The majority of people do not "think" at all in these matters—they only "think they think," and are in reality governed entirely by their feelings, emotions, desires and fears, modified and directed by the suggestions of the outside world.

The third phase of will is that of volition or action. In this phase the latent power of desire is released, in accordance with the decision made as above stated. The strength of the action depends upon the force of the desire, or the necessity of the action, the latter being but another form of desire, as you will see if you consider the matter for a moment. There is a point of hesitation before desire springs into will-action—the point

The Will

of indecision which occupies but a small fraction of a second of time; in fact, particularly among the lower and untrained examples of the race, the action is almost automatic and without rational consideration. Some desires never pass into the stage of action, but are held back either by the power of conflicting desires, or else from want of energy in the desire itself.

But in this, as in the other phases of mental action, The New Psychology does not content itself with a mere discourse upon the nature and action of the will—it proceeds to inform one how the will may be trained and applied to the best advantage. The training of the will properly forms the subject of a separate volume, and one of the books of this series will be devoted to it. But a few general rules may be given here, as follows:

I. The recognition of the Ego as master of the will. This recognition must be more than an abstract intellectual assent to the idea—it must consist of a conscious, intuitional feeling of the presence and reality of the "I" as the center of the mental field, and the master of the faculties, the feelings, the emotions, the desires, the imagination, the thoughts, the acts. The Ego must turn its attention and interest inward toward itself, and contemplate itself in a manner possible to no other act of contemplation. It must inwardly cognize itself as the "I"—an actual, living being, or entity. To do this the "I" must, for the moment and purpose, separate itself from the various instruments and attributes belonging to it—must see and feel itself simply as the pure Ego—the "I am." It may take some time and practice in order to bring about this realization and the sense of power that comes with it, but the time and effort are well worth while, and every step of the process brings with it power and a consciousness of mastery. Read the chapter dealing with the Ego, and apply the principles and ideas contained therein.

II. Practice the control of the other portions of the mind by the will under the direction of the Ego. *Will* to will. Then will that you feel and desire and think and act according to the idea first formed—an idea that should be consistent with your highest ideals and according to your highest reason and clearest judgment. You feel a desire to do or not to do a certain thing; here is your chance to prove your will. Deliberately determine that you *shall* desire and feel the exact opposite of your present desire, and then proceed to manifest in action that idea and determination. The desire or feeling will struggle and rebel—it will fight for life and continuance—but you must oppose to it the deadly cold steel of your will, as directed by the pure Ego. Persevere and yield not an inch—assert your mastery of our own mental domain. Ask no quarter and give none, and as sure as tomorrow's sun will rise, so surely will your will triumph, for it is positive to the mental states when properly applied and persistently exerted.

III. Cultivate the faculty of deliberation and consideration. In short, look before you leap. Test your feelings, emotions, impulses, and desires by the light of your reason. Test everything by the touch-stone: "Will this make me stronger? Does this make me more powerful? Does this tend toward attainment? Is this conducive to my highest good?" This does not necessarily mean that you should be afraid to act, and hesitate to make up your mind. Deliberation is often accomplished in the twinkling of an eye. The thing is to be sure that you *have* deliberated—sure that you have turned the light of understanding upon the impulse—sure that you have subjected the mental state to the conscious scrutiny of the Ego—instead of having merely acted from habit or impulse. *Be sure you know what you want*—and then do it. "Be sure you're right, then go ahead." Hold the wild horses of your chariot firmly in the hands of the Ego, whose reins and guiding lines are the will.

IV. Cultivate the attention until you can focus it upon an object or idea with concentrated force. The attention determines the path of the will—either toward or away from

The Will

the object of the attention, as the case may be. Attention is the eye of the Ego, the chariot driver.

V. Acquire the habit of controlling yourself by your will. When you have once acquired this habit, half the battle will be over, for the rest of the mind will have learned to respond to the guiding line and reins. The wild horses of the mind will have learned the effect of control and will interpose a constantly decreasing resistance. Don't allow your mental horses to run away with the chariot. These mental steeds will do wonderful work when controlled, but if allowed to pull along unrestrained and heedless of the hand of the master, will run you into mire and morass, and may wreck the chariot and throw the charioteer into the ditch or over the precipice.

VI. Train the mental steeds by driving them in directions contrary to those they may want to follow—this not because their way is necessarily wrong in such cases, but because you wish to train them to the use of the rein and curb—to accustom them to your mastery. One of the best ways to administer this kind of training is deliberately to make yourself perform some disagreeable task, something that you do not wish to do, or do not feel like doing. Here you will have a fight worthy of your mettle. The rebellious feelings and desires will rear and plunge and use every art and wile in order to defeat your purpose. Finding that you are determined to rule, they may even seemingly acquiesce only to take you by surprise and off your guard when you relax your efforts and believe that you have conquered. They sometimes act like Josh Billings' mule who stayed good three months in order to get a chance to kick the man. Desires and feelings are wily animals—watch them and do not be caught napping or off your guard. By doing disagreeable things once in a while—doing something that you do not feel like doing, and leaving undone something that you feel very much like doing, you will gain a control that will serve you well in some hour of need when you will require all of your will power in order to act right. The whole secret is teaching the desires the *habit* of being controlled by the will. Many great men have known this law, and have employed it advantageously. One writer mentions the case of a man who was found reading a dry book on political economy. His friend expressing surprise, he replied: "I am doing this because I dislike it." He was training his mental horses. One of the best and simplest methods of putting this rule into effect is to heed the popular adage: "Do It Now!" Procrastination is a particularly balky horse.

These several rules may appear very simple—so simple that many of you will be inclined to shrug your shoulders and murmur "Platitudes!" Platitudes they may be—but have you ever tried to practice them? That is the test of their real value—practice and actual trial. We say to you positively and with all the earnestness at our command: If you will but master these rules and make them your own, if you will but put them into actual practice for a single month, you will thank us over and over again for suggesting them to you; for you will find yourself a new man or woman, with new and greater powers than you had ever dreamed of possessing. And you will have opened up to yourself not only wonderful paths of power, but also wonderful paths of pleasure; for there is no enjoyment equal to that of the master who has learned to attain, accomplish and surmount natural obstacles. The joy of the victor in such a conflict more than repays him for his struggle. The man who masters himself is well on his way to master the things outside. One who masters himself has grasped the Key of Power.

In conclusion, we ask you to read these words of Halleck which bear directly upon this phase of the subject: "It is the function of a well-trained will to adhere to a given line of conduct or ideas, until they have become an integral part of the self. Only those ideas which are so absorbed become valuable elements of the character. We are coins, the metal of which has been dug from the mines of our inborn intellectual and moral faculties by will power. If we properly work these mines, we may find metal enough in us to justify a stamp of a very

The Will

high value. On the other hand, though there is much unmined metal beneath the surface, we often form a character marked with a penny stamp. It may be true that circumstances stamp us to a certain extent, but it is also true that the way in which we use them stamps us indelibly."

Do not remain the slave of circumstances, feelings, emotions, or desires—but assert yourself—your real self—the Ego—YOU.

Chapter XVI.

Thinking: Conscious and Subconscious.

There is no word used more frequently in connection with psychology than the one forming the first word of the title of this chapter. And yet how few people are able to define or explain the term. What is it to think! The dictionaries define the word "think" as follows: "To occupy the mind on some subject; to have ideas; to revolve ideas in the mind; to cogitate; to reason; to exercise the power of thought; to have a succession of ideas or intellectual states; to perform any mental operation; to muse; to meditate; to judge; to form a conclusion; to determine;" etc. Surely a comprehensive string of definitions—telling us but little. Halleck says: "To think is to compare things with each other, to notice wherein they agree or differ, and to classify them according to these agreements and differences. It enables us to put into a few classes the billions of things that strike our perceptive faculties; to tie things with like qualities into a bundle by themselves, and to infer that what is true of one of these things will be true of the others without actual experience in each individual case; and to introduce law and order into what at first seemed a mass of chaotic materials."

It is not our purpose in this work to enter into a technical examination of the various processes of thinking, describing

The New Psychology

the various processes of forming concepts in their phases of presentation of materials, comparison of materials, abstract consideration, generalization, and denomination; or the processes of judgment; or the various processes of reasoning, with the laws of thought and principles of logic—these things are very important, but the ordinary text-books go into detail regarding them. Our concern in this chapter is solely with the additional light that The New Psychology has to throw upon the work of thinking.

You will readily see that in all thinking processes the subconscious mind supplies the bulk of the material for the thought—the raw material from which the finished product of thought is manufactured. Without this material there could be no such thing as thought as we know it, for without the great subconscious storehouse of memory upon which to draw there could be no comparison or classification, no grouping or assorting, no gathering together of experienced sensations or perceptions in order to form ideas. Without the subconscious memory the mind of man would always be that of the infant. It is readily admitted that the man should be able to think better upon any given subject upon which he has been educated or instructed, than a man of equal mental power who lacks that education or instruction. But where are the results of that education or instruction stored for use? In the subconscious memory, of course. Deprive the man of his memory of the instruction or education, and he sinks to the level of the uneducated and uninstructed man. This is true of all branches of instruction, from the blacking of boots to higher mathematics or philosophy. The material for thought is always stored in the subconscious regions of the mind.

The following quotations from leading authorities will show you that the above statements are warranted. Bacon says: "All knowledge is but remembrance." Emerson says: "Memory is a primary and fundamental faculty, without which none other can work; the cement, the bitumen, the matrix in which the other faculties are imbedded. Without it all life and thought were an unrelated succession." Burke says: "There is no faculty of the mind which can bring its energy into effect unless the memory is stored with ideas for it to look upon." Helvetius says: "Memory is the magazine in which are deposited the sensations, facts and ideas, whose different combinations form knowledge." Dr. Johnson said: "Memory is the purveyor of reason." Hamilton says: "Memory is the Power of retaining knowledge in the mind, but out of consciousness."

The above quotations refer to memory, but memory is but one of the incidents of the subconscious region of the mind. Memory is but a function of the subconscious mentality. Memory is but a term applied to the subconscious storehouse of which we have spoken in previous chapters. The working of the subconscious mentality is manifested when we consider the next step, that of recollection and remembrance. There is a great difference between these two terms, although they are often considered as synonyms. Locke, in his celebrated work *"Essay Concerning Human Understanding,"* clearly points out the distinction, saying: "...regarding the power to revive in our minds those ideas which, after imprinting, have disappeared, or have been laid aside out of sight.... When an idea again recurs, *without the operation of the like object* on the external sensory, it is Remembrance; if it is sought after by the mind, and with pain and endeavor found, and brought again into view, it is Recollection."

Now it is just this distinction between Remembrance and Recollection, as made by Locke, that brings out the several operations of the mind in thinking, as taught by The New Psychology. We are fully familiar with that laborious effort to re-collect the scattered bits of information, ideas, impressions, perceptions, etc., in our concentrated thought upon any subject. This is the ordinary method of thought as practiced by the average thinker. It is a will-tiring process, requiring the utmost powers of concentration and attention in order to get the best results. It is, indeed, a task of "pain and endeavor," as Locke expresses it, and yet the average man thinks that it is the only way possible in the processes of ordinary thought. The most annoying part of the process is that so much time, attention and concentration are necessary to bring together the simplest elements of the thought. It is this gathering of the little things that is the hardest work in the processes of thought.

Startling as it may appear to those unacquainted with the idea, The New Psychology offers an improvement upon the old processes—an improvement bearing the same relation to the old processes that Remembrance bears to Recollection, as defined by Locke. In other words, the subconscious mentality may be trained to do much of the work—the drudgery, in fact—that is usually performed by the conscious mentality. The subconsciousness will soon learn to perform much of the drudgery and detail work of bringing together the scattered bits of mental impressions, arranging them in convenient groups and parcels, classifying them in such manner as to render them easy to use. And all this without the "pain and endeavor" attendant upon efforts of consciousness—for the subconscious mentality does not tire as does the conscious, no effort of attention being required in its processes—leaving the conscious mind free to think of other things in the meantime, and to be fresh and active to make the necessary arrangements, deductions, judgments, determinations and conclusions when the results of the subconscious operations finally reach the field of consciousness. You think this strange, and a bit of "wild theory" perhaps. But it is not. In fact, it is but a bit of mental work that is going on all the time with many persons, and yet only in a small degree compared with the possibilities of its employment when directed and commanded by the will, and trained by practice and exercise. Let us see what the authorities have to say on this subject.

In our chapter on the Subconsciousness we showed you that a very large percentage of the work of mentation was performed

Thinking: Conscious and Subconscious

below the field of consciousness. We quoted you many authorities bearing out this truth. But we did not give you any examples of the actual employment of the subconsciousness in the process of thinking. Therefore we now call your attention to the testimony of several well-known writers on the subject, in order to show you that this is not merely a bit of fanciful theorizing without a basis of fact.

Thompson says: "At times I have had a feeling of the uselessness of all voluntary effort, and also that the matter was working itself clear in my mind. It has many times seemed to me that I was really a passive instrument in the hands of a person not myself. Because of having to wait for the results of these unconscious processes, I have proved the habit of getting together material in advance, and then leaving the mass to digest itself till I am ready to write about it. I delayed for a month the writing of my book 'System of Psychology,' but continued reading the authorities. I would not try to think about the book. I would watch with interest the people passing the windows. One evening when reading the paper, the substance of the missing part of the book flashed upon my mind, and I began to write. This is only a sample of many such experiences."

Berthelot, the eminent chemist, has said: "The experiments leading to my discoveries have never been the result of carefully followed trains of thought—of pure reasoning processes—but have come of themselves, so to speak, from the clear sky." Mozart said: "I cannot say that I can account for my composition. My ideas flow, and I cannot say whence or how they come. I do not hear in my imagination the parts successively, but I hear them, as it were, all at once. The rest is merely an attempt to reproduce what I have heard." Another writer says: "In writing this book, I have been unable to arrange my knowledge of a subject for days and weeks, until I experienced a clearing up of my mind, when I took my pen and unhesitatingly wrote the result. I have best accomplished this by leading the conscious mind as far as possible from the subject upon which I was writing."

The New Psychology

Another writer has recorded instances of what he calls "unconscious rumination," occurring in cases when he was considering ideas opposed to his customary ones. At first he was unable to assimilate the new ideas with his old ones, but he would then lay aside the matter from active consideration for a period of time extending over several days, or even weeks and months. When he would bring the matter again into his field of consciousness, he would find that the matter had been threshed out in his subconsciousness, and a new arrangement and classification made, a new grouping arranged, and the entire matter was presented to him in logical sequence and order, just as a careful compiler of a digest would have arranged and ordered it.

The later works on the subject of subconscious mentation contain many instances and examples of the kind above related. But nearly all speak as if the matter were out of relation to the will of the individual, and "just happened." In the majority of the cases referred to in the books, some of which have been given above, the effort of remembrance, arrangement, and adjustment performed by the subconsciousness was undoubtedly set in operation in response to the strong desire of the individual operation along subconscious lines. But the same effect, and even greater, may be obtained if the desire is accompanied by a positive command of the will to the subconsciousness, along the lines of auto-suggestion, to the effect that the desired work be performed. The subconsciousness is peculiarly amenable to suggestion and command, and if the individual will acquire the art of *willing* that the subconscious mentality gather together the scattered materials in its region, and bring together, combine, and arrange all the material it can find within itself concerning the particular subject or object, it will do so.

When the matter is again brought into the field of consciousness, the individual will find to his surprise that he knows a great deal more about that particular subject than he did before. Perhaps it may be necessary to refer the matter back

Thinking: Conscious and Subconscious

to the subconsciousness several times before the desired result is obtained, but a little progress will be noted each time. Then again, it is largely a matter of practice and "knack." After one acquires the method, he will find a most faithful ally and helper in his subconsciousness, which is not only willing but glad to perform the mental drudgery for him. This help is akin to that of a faithful assistant which will gather the various materials for a task, or operation, and place them before his chief, arranged in careful order and grouping that the chief may proceed to put the finishing touches of selection, determination and final judgment on the whole. For the details of using auto-suggestion, we refer you to the chapter on that subject.

Chapter XVII.

Mental Suggestion.

THE WORD "suggestion" in its common acceptation means "a hint, an intimation," etc. But the use of the word by psychologists during the last twenty years has given to it a secondary meaning quite distinct from the original. In psychology the word "suggestion" means an impression made upon the mind, or attempted to be made upon the mind, which is more in the nature of a subtle hint or intimation than a rational or logical appeal to the judgment. In an argument or logical appeal there is evident a desire to convince or convert the intellect of the hearer, while in suggestion there is rather an attempt made to *insinuate* the keen edge of an idea into the feeling or emotional region of his mind—into his subconsciousness, in fact. In argument there is the desire to convince—to bring around the mind of the hearer to see the logical and rational weight of the ideas presented. But in suggestion there is simply the desire to arouse the feeling side, or else subtly to implant the idea into the subconscious mentality of the hearer without having it subjected to the test of experience or reason, so that when it afterward emerges into the field of consciousness it may be thought to be the original thought, idea or feeling of the thinker himself. This form of suggestion is generally known as Mental Suggestion, in order to distinguish it from the ordinary "suggestion," although there is but the difference of degree between the two.

We are constantly accepting suggestions from our environment, the degree and character of the same depending materially upon the degree of employment of the judgment and will of the individual. We receive the greater part of our education from the suggestions of those around us in childhood. Suggestion, in this sense, is quite proper, and has its place in our mental life. It is only when we open ourselves to suggestion from outside, without interposing our judgment or individuality, that we suffer ourselves to be unduly influenced. For extreme suggestibility is undoubtedly a surrender of the individuality. The less individuality the person manifests the greater is his degree of receptivity to suggestions. The man deficient in individuality lets others do his thinking for him, and accepts the dicta of others as proven truth and allows the impression to be formed in his subconsciousness, whence it emerges as his own thought. Very few people think for themselves. They allow others to formulate ideas for them, and to express them in catchphrases, etc., which the negative person appropriates and repeats, thinking that he is uttering the results of his own thought. There are several general forms of suggestion, a glance at which will enable you better to appreciate the importance of mental suggestion in every-day life.

There are four general phases or classes of Mental Suggestion, as follows:

I. Suggestion of Authority.
II. Suggestion of Imitation.
III. Suggestion of Association.
IV. Suggestion of Repetition.

Suggestion of Authority is the impression made upon the minds of persons by others speaking with real or assumed authority, which gives to their utterances weight out of proportion to their rational value. When one whose authority is accepted speaks with firmness and an air of conviction, he will have many people to accept his words and ideas at their face value without subjecting them to the test of their judgment. So important is the effect produced by the appearance of authority that unscrupulous persons have managed to impose on many good people simply by an impudent assumption and air of authority, without the real basis for their claims, and the people have accepted their statement and claims without question. The proper carriage, an air of gravity, and a manner of importance, will impose upon many people the suggestion of authority, and henceforth whatever is uttered is accepted without question. The history of the false religious impostors of all ages show the importance of this form of suggestion. And this is quite as much in evidence to-day as one hundred or five hundred years ago.

Some man or woman assumes the air of authority, and speaks in a "Thus saith the Lord" manner, and lo! he or she has thousands of human sheep following after, and giving up their hard earned money to swell the coffers of the "apostle" or "prophet." So true is this, that many persons undoubtedly insane have assumed the authoritative air and had their thousands of sincere followers. Suggestible people seldom ask: "What does my reason and judgment inform me regarding this thing." Instead they ask "What does Mr. So-and-so, or Mrs. This-and-that, say about it?" They are constantly seeking the voice of authority, instead of using and developing their own thinking machines. They discourage individuality rather than encourage it.

Individualistic persons do not hesitate to avail themselves of the knowledge of other persons who have had experience along the desired lines, but they always use their judgment in deciding whether these other persons really do know, and never accept the mere appearance and manner of authority for the real thing. They are like the man from Missouri, in the current slang phrase—they say: "You'll have to *show me*." And when they receive the opinions of the others, they carefully weigh and test them. The world is full of "confidence men" in all walks of life, who impose upon their fellows by reason of this Suggestion of Authority. Apply the test of Individuality and reason, and their power departs. In realizing the "I," one assumes a positive mental attitude toward others which in itself is an air of authority, which neutralizes the pinchbeck imitations.

The second form of mental suggestion is the Suggestion of Imitation. Animals and human beings are imitative creatures, and a large proportion of their thoughts, ideas and actions are caused by the example of others. We hear people all around us saying that such and such a thing is so, and we take it for granted without testing it with our judgment and reason. It is the authority of the crowd, often based on no truer foundation than the authority of some individual. We follow our leaders by imitation as well as by authority. Let some old sheep jump over a low fence, and the whole flock follows—and keeps on jumping even though the rails of the fence be removed. The authority and power of fashion is derived through this phase of suggestion. We want to do as the rest are doing, although we can give no rational excuse for so doing. Let a man stand on a crowded sidewalk and stare up at a skyscraper, and immediately hundreds are doing the same thing, and a large crowd gathers until the police disperse them. Let some one in a streetcar begin to shiver, and in a few moments every one is complaining how chilly the car is, and beginning to turn up his coat collar. And so it goes—human sheep we are to a great extent. It is only when we begin to assert our individuality that we are disposed to act upon our own judgment instead of that of the crowd. Crowds are very suggestible, and often do things that the separate persons composing them would not think of doing. The history of mobs and crowd-hysteria gives us ample proof of this. Do your own thinking, judging and deciding—

according to the best that is in you, and after considering the best that is outside of you. But do not become a human sheep.

The third phase or class of mental suggestion is the Suggestion of Association. This form of suggestion operates by reason of the association of certain outward appearances with certain inward characteristics or facts. We are used to seeing a preacher act in a certain manner. Let some impostor come along who has the facial characteristics and the dress of the preacher, and we act toward him as if he were the real article. We confuse the appearances with the reality. In this way we allow the outward appearances, manner, and words of people to suggest to us certain facts or ideas which may be entirely absent. We mistake the shadow for the substance—the symbol for the reality.

The secret of the actor and orator lies largely in the employment of this phase of suggestion. They use the words and tones connected with certain emotions and feelings, and thus induce or reproduce the appropriate feelings in our minds. Our subconsciousness becomes the key-board of a mental piano upon which the deft fingers of the speaker may play any tune he chooses—if we allow him to do so. Similarly, scenes and objects connected with certain feelings and emotions tend to arouse in us the original feelings associated with them. Black clothing of a certain kind is associated with funerals—orange blossoms with weddings—certain styles of architecture with certain things. In short, the world is full of symbols associated in our minds with certain ideas, feelings, emotions,—and unless we understand the law of suggestion we allow these symbols to play upon us, consciously or unconsciously—either without or with the purpose of other people—until we become little more than responsive phonographs giving forth the sounds indicated by the records placed in them.

The antidote lies in the recognition of the law. When once you realize how your feelings, emotions and ideas may be aroused by means of the outside symbols of words, objects, scenes, sounds, odors, etc., then you will be on your guard and will learn to smile and lay aside the induced feeling or idea with the remark: "This is simply a suggestion through association." But on the contrary, one may surround himself with the associations calculated to bring out the best in him, and to avoid those calculated to bring out the undesirable qualities—the law works in both ways, remember. The associations connected with a library, and a bar-room, induce totally opposite feelings and ideas, as you know—this is the key-note.

The fourth phase or class of mental suggestion is the Suggestion of Repetition. This depends upon the well-known psychological fact that "Suggestion gains force through repetition." Hear a thing often enough and you grow to accept it as truth. Tell a lie often enough, and you get to believe it yourself. The subconsciousness receives all accepted impressions; and each repetition tends to make the impression deeper and clearer. The great advertisers of the country depend upon this law of suggestion through repetition for fastening their statements in your mind. You see a positive statement or "direct command" of some advertiser repeated over and over again in every paper, periodical or magazine, as well as on the train signs and the bill-boards—and before long it is fastened in your mind. The phrase: "Jollyman's Soap is the *Best* soap!" if repeated constantly day in and day out in every possible way, would convince a large percentage of the people that it *is* the best soap—they would not stop to argue the question—here would be the effect of an authoritative, direct and positive suggestion constantly repeated until accepted.

In this short space we cannot begin to do more than call your attention to the general principles of mental suggestion, and to put you on your guard regarding it. Remember always that the best of us are more or less affected by mental suggestions along all of the lines mentioned above. The thing to do is, first, to develop our individuality until we realize what real thoughts and feelings are like; then to master them along the lines of The New Psychology; then to distinguish outside suggestions, and

Mental Suggestion

accept only those conducive to our best interests, rejecting the others; and finally to turn the law to our own advantage, and to surround ourselves so far as possible with the best suggestive influences, avoiding the other kind so far as is possible—in this way we take advantage of the law instead of allowing it to use us. The well-poised individual who realizes the "I" is not apt to be influenced by many suggestions that easily induce feelings and ideas in persons who lack this realization. The consciousness of the "I" renders one positive to outside influence of a negative nature. To explain "just why" would involve us in a long explanation that would carry us across the line of philosophy—enough to know that it is so, and that you may prove the fact yourself if you will but try. The proof of the pudding is in the eating; and an ounce of proven fact is worth more than a pound of statement.

Chapter XVIII.

Auto-Suggestion.

An "auto-suggestion" is a mental suggestion made to oneself *by* oneself. It is a case of "sez I to meself, sez I." And strange to say, the effect of the thought of oneself shaped into words and directed to oneself is charged with a dynamic force far in excess of the same thought merely "held" in the mind and not so expressed. Strange, isn't it? There is added to an expressed thought a something dynamic, vital, forceful, and active that is absent from the thought that is merely "held" in the mind. The expression imparts a vital force to the thought that it did not possess before. And this is true in cases in which the expression is made to oneself, as well as when it is made to others. The same law is evoked. A latent thought is static—an expressed thought is dynamic. Therein lies the force and value of auto-suggestion.

In the various cults of the "new thought" we have heard much regarding "holding the thought," which means that an idea constantly kept before the mind has a tendency to materialize into outward reality and expression. This is very well in its way, and is based upon psychological principles, but there is a more active force in thought, which was at first overlooked—but not for long. The followers of the "new thought" teachings soon began to hear much regarding "affirmations," "statements," "declarations," and the like. These statements, etc., were modeled upon the ancient Hindu mantrams or sacred statements, and were held to be very efficacious in producing results. To many these methods seemed either ridiculous, or else weird and mysterious, according to the viewpoint of the observer. But the students of The New Psychology see nothing ridiculous in these methods, although often the exaggeration of the statement verges upon the ridiculous. And they see nothing weird or mysterious in the procedure, either, for they recognized the working of their old friend Suggestion, or, rather, auto-suggestion, in these methods—it is simply another case of the added force of expressed thought—another instance of "sez I to meself, sez I"—with the natural result.

The student of The New Psychology sees in all of the various forms of "new-thought" statements, affirmations, declarations,—all auto-suggestions, in fact—the working of this law of expressed thought in its effect upon the subconscious mentality. He sees in each statement of "I am this," or "I am that," an expressed idea directed to one's own subconsciousness, there to be recorded and preserved just as are the impressions of outside suggestions. The man who starts out by saying: "I am courageous," in the right spirit, and who keeps pegging away at the same auto-suggestion, day after day, always, however, keeping the spirit in the words, cannot escape changing his subconscious mentality in accordance with his statements. He will make his statements come true, if he goes about it in the right way, and persists in the right spirit. And, likewise, the man who is always saying "The world is against me; I am a failure," and repeating the statement to himself, over and over, day after day, will surely create for himself such a mental attitude and personality as will inevitably tend to make of him what he is stating that he is.

To those who have not looked into the matter carefully, there is a tendency to decry the value of these self-statements, particularly after witnessing some extreme instance in the person of some fanatical follower of the cults. He is apt to smile at the whole matter, and dismiss it with a "There's nothing to it." But let the same man seriously contemplate the results of some of his friends starting in a course of "I am a failure" line of auto-suggestions, in earnest and repeatedly,—let him imagine such an occurrence, and he will readily say: "Why, that would ruin a fellow in no time." He would see the application of the negative auto-suggestions in a moment. Well, the same rule applies in both cases. It is a poor rule that will not work both ways. Leaving out of the question the absurd extravagances of some of the cults, it is a psychological fact that a line of positive auto-suggestions, intelligently applied, and faithfully kept up, will surely produce changes in the character, personality, and mental quality of the person making them. It is possible for one literally to "make himself over," mentally, by an intelligent course of auto-suggestion. To all of the methods and exercises given in this book for the mastery; and control of the mental faculties by the will of the Ego, there may well be added the use of auto-suggestions along the same lines. The plan of "talking up" to one's mental faculties works like a charm, for it is but the adding of dynamic force to the idea—it is a form of expression into activity.

You may hold the thought that you are going to say "No!" to a question or proposition that you know will be submitted to you during the day. You may make up your mind firmly to take the necessary position and attitude. But when you say to yourself, in actual words: "I shall say No! and stick to it no matter what happens"—saying it in a tone conveying positive conviction and determination—then you have done much to clinch the matter. And if you will add to this a mental picture of yourself saying and acting in accordance therewith, you will have done much to make a mental path easy to follow. That is what the auto-suggestion does—it makes a mental path—

it establishes a habit line of action—and you know what that means if you have read this book.

In some of my writings I have recommended that the person making the auto-suggestion not only content himself with saying "I am (or I will do) so and so," but also "talk up" to himself, calling himself by name and saying "See here, John Smith, you are going to do so and so," or "you *are* so-and-so." This plan brings into effect the positive character of actual suggestion from outside—suggestion of authority. One may, in this way, use all the methods of mental suggestion upon himself, and obtain the benefits that arise from positive suggestions from good authorities. One may order himself to be what he wills himself to be, along the lines of auto-suggestion, with good results. For what is this auto-suggestion, after all, if not the assertion of the Ego of its mastery and control over its mental states—the creation of new mental states, and building up of new characteristics, powers, and personality? The Ego is the suggester of the auto-suggestion when properly used. It is right along with the other teachings of The New Psychology.

Every person is largely what he is by reason of the things that he has said about himself, or else acquiesced in when others said them about him. He has been filling himself with auto-suggestions since he was a small child, and his subconsciousness is filled with these impressions, and is constantly passing them up to the field of consciousness, and manifesting them in action. Just as the suggestions of others have registered themselves and then played their part in character building, so have the opinions expressed about oneself had much to do with the formation of one's character. Of course people are not always that which they say to themselves they are, nevertheless the latter has had its formative effect and creative action. And, after all, a man does not always say to himself, about himself, that which he says to others about himself. You will find that many a man does not hold himself as highly as his outward statements would indicate. Many

Auto-Suggestion

a blusterer has said to himself, when alone: "Smith, you are a coward and a fool"—and the auto-suggestion was impressed on his mind according to the degree of belief in it.

A man does considerable "talking to himself," although his words may never be spoken aloud. He forms his thoughts into words, often, and says them to himself just as truly as if he were to speak them aloud. And these things have an effect upon him. It is not wise to admit weakness to oneself. It is all very well to preserve an honesty and integrity toward oneself, as well as toward others, but one should avoid the "I can't" self-confession as much as possible. One should treat his mind always as if it were capable of great things, and as if it were going to improve and increase its efficiency. Never give your mind auto-suggestions of a negative nature, any more than you would give them to someone in your employ from whom you expected to get good work. Set your mind aside as an employé or helper, and know your Ego as Yourself. Then say and do toward your mind the things that you would do toward your employé. Tell it what you want done; what results you expect it to accomplish; and in other ways treat it as does the wise employer in the case of an efficient employé. Don't abuse it, of course, although a good straight talking to will not be amiss at times. Never tell it that it is worthless, but always hold up to it the ideal of better things that are possible to it, and that you expect from it.

All of this may seem absurd to those who are not acquainted with the psychological principles involved. It is a matter of the employment and treatment of the subconscious mentality, first, last and all the time. It is bringing to your aid those tiny workers of the subconscious region, who are ready to work for you if only you will instruct them and inform them of what you want done. Those who have studied the previous chapters of this book should experience no difficulty in understanding the reasons behind the phenomena of auto-suggestion. And now that you have had your attention directed toward the subject, you will be able to explain to your own satisfaction much that may have perplexed you in the "affirmations," "statements," "declarations," etc., of the cults. There is nothing weird or mysterious about the matter—except that everything about the mind is mysterious, at the last—it is but the application of the power of the Ego over the subconscious regions of its mental kingdom.

Chapter XIX.

Mind and Body.

The New Psychology takes into active account the influence of the mind upon the body. The older psychology devoted but scant attention to this very important phase of the general subject, evidently regarding it as but an interesting side issue, rather than as a vital feature of the main subject. It has long been recognized that mental states react upon physical conditions, either favorably or adversely, according to the nature of the mental states. But the older psychologists contented themselves with noting the facts, somewhat grudgingly in some cases, without attempting to point out methods whereby the mental force could be used to promote health and restore normal conditions, or else to prevent the production of abnormal conditions by restraining adverse mental states. But with the entry of The New Psychology into the field, the therapeutic value of the mental forces came prominently to the fore.

The casual investigator of the subject of the influence of mental states over physical conditions and psychological functioning is very apt to be "side-tracked" by the claims of the various creeds, cults and schools of the day, with the several religious, metaphysical and occult theories and doctrines. He may see cures of physical ills being made by the teachers or healers of certain cults—he may easily prove the genuineness of such cures—and then, seeing this, he is apt to accept the same as a proof of the theories of doctrines advanced by those making the cures. But a wider field of investigation will reveal to him the surprising fact that other cults, schools and creeds are also making the same kind of cures in the same kind of cases, and in the same proportion—although the several doctrines, theories and beliefs of these schools may vary greatly, and are often diametrically opposed to each other. A careful analysis of the results of a wide investigation of mental healing will lead the student to the conviction that all of these various schools and cults are employing some common universal principle, having nothing whatever to do with the respective religious, metaphysical, or occult teachings of the several schools and cults. In other words, they make their cures in spite of their doctrines and theories, and not because of them. Of course the advocates of the several cults and schools vigorously combat this position, but the facts remain apparent to the disinterested investigator who manages to keep himself clear of the entanglements of attractions of all the schools and cults. The question then arises: What is this fundamental principle?

We believe that a full and complete answer to the above question is impossible unless we are able to ascertain the nature of mind itself. This knowledge not being possessed at this stage of man's evolution, the first question cannot be fully answered. The best we can do is to attach a name to the principle as seen at work, and then discover the "how" of its application, leaving the "why" to dwell with the other unanswered "whys" of science. The best authorities have agreed in using the term "mental suggestion," or "mental induction," in speaking of the working principle of the effect of mind upon physical states. It is true that we are unable to answer the question: "But what is Mental Suggestion, at the last!" But at least we are able to tell how to use it, and what are its effects. We also are able to ascertain, by experiments, the fact that the phenomena are in some way bound up with the subconscious mind. Some hold that the subconscious mind exerts an influence over all of the physical organs and parts, and others (including ourselves) are now advancing the idea that in every portion of the body, down to the smallest cell, there exists "mind" of some degree, and that these "minds" of the parts are related to the great subconscious region of the mind of the individual. But this is merely a matter of the detail of theories. The fact remains that we may *act* as if there was mind in every cell and part of the body, and that this "mind" of the parts is amenable to suggestion or commands from the central mind of the individual, or that of other persons. The process in either case comes under the head of Suggestion.

Physiologists have observed that mental states affect the digestion, and therefore the entire physical condition of the body. There have been cases in which conditions have rendered it possible actually to observe the operations of the digestive organs, and the experiments showed that grief, anger, fear, or worry retarded the digestive processes, and if sufficiently extreme actually stopped them entirely. Every physiologist knows that cheerfulness and hope increase the physical being like a tonic, while the opposite states depress the system and lower the vitality. Hope and cheerfulness are the two best tonics known to science, and the reverse states will lower the vitality to such a degree that often the tide may be turned in favorable cases, and death result. Ill people have recovered upon the receipt of good news, while fright and fear have killed their thousands. People have died under the belief that they have taken poison, when in fact they had not done so. Fear and worry have checked the flow of milk in the breasts of nursing women. All sorts of imaginary virtues have been bestowed upon certain religious relics, holy places, etc., in all religions, and thousands of cures have resulted therefrom— merely the effect of the mental suggestion. Imagination has an undoubted powerful therapeutic value recognized and applied by physicians who appreciate the fact.

Dr. Richardson says: "The passions which act most severely on the physical life are anger, fear, hatred, and grief. The other passions are comparatively innocuous....Of all the passions I have enumerated as most detrimental to life, anger stands first. He is a man very rich indeed in physical power who can afford to be angry. The richest cannot afford it many times without insuring the penalty, a penalty that is always severe....We say that a man was 'red' with rage, by which term, as by degrees of comparison, we express the extent of his fury. Physiologically, we are then speaking of the nervous condition of the minute circulation of his blood: that 'red' rage means partial paralysis of minute blood-vessels; that 'white' rage means temporary suspension of the action of the prime mover of the circulation itself. But such disturbances cannot often be produced without the occurrence of permanent organic evils of the vital organs, especially of the heart and of the brain."

Dr. Hack Tuke a number of years ago wrote a very interesting work showing the therapeutic effect of the "imagination." By "imagination" he meant the mental action that is brought into effect by what is now called mental suggestion. He gave a number of very interesting cases that had come under his personal observation, all of which tended to show the great dynamic force of the "imagination," or rather of the mental states induced by mental suggestion. Dr. Tuke was one of the first persons to make a scientific claim of the influence of the mental states upon the physical functions, and he really laid the foundations for the experimental work that followed and which is now embodied in this phase of The New Psychology. Among other things he said: "There is no sensation, whether general or special, excited by agents acting upon the body from without, which cannot be excited also from within by emotional states affecting the sensory centers, such sensations being referred by the mind to the point at which sthe nerves terminate in the body." He also approvingly quoted the statement of the celebrated physician, Dr. John Hunter, who said: "I am confident that I can fix my attention to any part, until I have a sensation in that part," Tuke adding: "These words should be inscribed in letters of gold over the entrance of a Hospital for the Cure of Disease by Psychopathy." He also said: "Thought strongly directed to any part tends to increase its vascularity, and consequently its sensibility."

And so you see, that the effect of mind upon body is a well established psychological and physiological fact, and does not depend upon any vague theory, creed, dogma or doctrine of any metaphysical, religious, or occult sect, cult, or school. It is a scientific principle not connected in any way with occultism, religion, or metaphysics, although all of these may furnish excellent channels or instruments for its employment. The stronger the degree of faith, hope and confident expectation aroused in the mind of the person, the better are the chances of a cure.

The subject of psychological therapy belongs to a special branch of The New Psychology, and we shall not attempt to go into details regarding it in this book. We have merely wished to direct your attention to the matter, that you may recognize its importance and give it its place in your mind. In a general way, however, we may say that every one may avail himself of the general principle by following the advice given in the previous part of this chapter. By cultivating the positive emotions of confidence, hope, courage, cheerfulness and good will, you may raise the vitality and general tone of your physical system so that it will be much better equipped to resist the attack of disease. And not a small part of this result is accomplished by the fact that in so doing you shut out or inhibit the negative emotions and feelings that go so far toward producing disease, or at least render the resisting powers of the system lower, so that disease more readily obtains a foothold. By establishing the habit of Right Thinking, you raise a powerful barrier against disease.

Not only is this so, but by properly directing the attention to parts of the body that are not functioning normally, you may obtain a certain control over them and obtain a response to your commands to them. By using the imagination to picture the desired normal condition, and then using the will to command the organ or part to conform to that ideal condition, you set in motion the dynamic force of that which is called "mental suggestion," and the psychological process is transmuted into a physiological process. In this brief statement is to be found the kernel of all mental healing; metaphysical healing; divine science, or any other form whereby the mind is exerted to regulate and control the physical functions. The rest is all a matter of detail, and "fringe."

Chapter XX.

Positive and Negative Qualities.

There seems to be a universal law of polarity—everything has its positive and negative aspects or poles. The mind is no exception to this rule. There are positive qualities of mind, and negative qualities of mind. The positive qualities or states manifest strength and power; the negative, weakness and impotence. There are two sides to every individual, and upon his decision between them depends his advancement, welfare, progress, and success. As Goethe says: "In my breast, alas, two souls dwell, all there is unrest. Each with the other strives for mastery, each from the other struggles to be free."

When the individual is forced to consider any feeling, emotion, idea, action, advice, suggestion or teaching, he should always submit it to the touch-stone of Positivity, by asking himself: *"Will this make me stronger; more powerful; more capable; more efficient; better?"* In the degree that the thing corresponds to these qualifications, so is its degree of positivity.

It becomes the duty of every individual wishing to progress on the path of Life, and desiring to become more proficient and capable in his expression and manifestation of mentality, to cultivate the positive qualities of the mind, and to restrain and inhibit the negative ones. This is the idea that we have carried with us through the course of writing the preceding chapters of this book. Behind every explanation, method, and bit of information, there has been always this one idea—the cultivation and development of your positive qualities, and the restraint and inhibition of your negative ones. And this is the test that we invite and urge you to make your rule of life when coming to the point of considering any feeling, emotion, thought or action—any mental state, in fact—this magic-test question: "*Will this make me stronger; more powerful; more capable; more efficient; better?*"

There is no trouble in any individual deciding which of his mental states or qualities are positive, and which are negative. Every one, if honest with himself, recognizes both sets of qualities within himself, and recognizes the different degrees of positivity and negativity, respectively, possessed by each particular one. It does not need a teacher to state that Courage is positive, and Cowardice negative; nor that Honesty is positive and Dishonesty negative; nor that Truth is positive, and Untruth negative; nor that Energy is positive and Slothfulness negative; nor that Persistence is positive, and the lack of it negative; and so on. One may almost intuitively place the tag of positivity or negativity upon these qualities or mental states without the need of a long list of them.

In the consideration of this matter you should always remember that every positive quality has its negative opposite. This is an invariable rule, and one that you may test for yourself. And arising from it is the important rule of The New Psychology that "*To develop a positive quality, it is important to restrain or inhibit its opposing negative; To restrain or inhibit a negative quality, develop and encourage its opposing positive.*" You will find constant reference to this leading rule in this book, for it is the foundation stone of the practical work of The New Psychology. It is worthy of being carved over the door of every institute of learning in the world, for its observance would

Positive and Negative Qualities

create a new race of men and women, and a new civilization of positive, capable, efficient people.

Beginning with our statement of the conception of the Ego, and its mastery and control over the mind, we began to urge upon you the cultivation of the positive qualities and the restraint of the negative ones. This is the first work of the Ego of the advancing man. The Ego should always be held positive to the feelings, emotions, desires, and other mental states. The will should be held positive to the desires. The Intellect should be held positive to the emotions, desires and feelings. The Ego should hold itself positive toward the subconsciousness in order that the latter shall be a faithful servant instead of a tyrannical master. The Ego should be positive toward the Attention and Imagination. And all this in order that the positive qualities of the individual may be developed instead of the negative ones; and that the negative qualities may be restrained or inhibited. To this end the entire work of this book is devoted. This is the meaning and reason of The New Psychology, not only to instruct the student along the lines of practical psychology, but also to instruct him that he *can* develop the positive, and restrain the negative qualities of his mind; and then to tell him how to do it.

To attain the desired positive state, the knowledge of the reality of the Ego has been stated to you. To know the Ego is to use it. And to use it is to acquire positivity. True Egoism develops positivity, while Egotism develops negativity, for it is in itself negative, being based on a false sense of the importance of personality instead of on the firm, real basis of individuality. The truth regarding consciousness is useful only in so far as we use the principles of controlling and developing it. The subconsciousness is a field for the highest and greatest endeavors of the race, in the direction of filling it with the thoughts, ideas, experiences and truths calculated to result and manifest in positive feeling, thought, and acting. The superconscious region is valuable to us only in the degree that it serves us and enables us to develop and advance.

The New Psychology

The principles regarding Impressions and Perception are important to us, because by controlling them we may acquire the qualities calculated to render us more efficient and capable. Every sense and every channel of impression and perception should be, and may be, devoted to the cultivation of the positive qualities, and to the restraint of the negative ones. By treading the right Mental Paths we acquire the habit of Right Thinking and Right Acting—both positive qualities. The truth of "as a man thinketh" is applicable to the cultivation of the positive qualities, and a restraint of the opposite ones. In the control of the Emotions we have a mighty instrument for the cultivation of the positive qualities. In the mastery and conscious control of the Imagination we have another powerful instrument. In the understanding of the nature of Desire and its management we have another. In the Will we have the reins that guide the fiery steeds of Desire, Emotion, and Feeling, and which may direct and guide them toward the righthand path—the path of positivity. In Mental Suggestion and Auto-Suggestion we have the methods whereby the Ego may control, develop and manage the mental faculties with a minimum of effort. In the management and control of Thought, we have the key toward the cultivation of the higher positive expressions and manifestations. And so, in each of the various parts and chapters of this book we have touched upon points concerning this question of positivity—have traveled the several roads leading toward the same goal—positivity.

Man should be more than a mere creature of chance, environment and outside influences. He should be ruled from within—self-ruled—by the power of the Ego. Instead of being merely a weak instrument of desire, emotion, and feeling, influenced by suggestions and impressions from every passing thing or person, man should be a strong instrument of the will guided and directed by the Ego. With full qualities of reason regulating, deciding and determining, and with full will enforcing the determination, man should become a very giant

Positive and Negative Qualities

of endeavor and attainment, instead of the petty, crawling, weakling that so many of his kind are now. Man has it in his power to make of himself what he will—to become his own mental creator, instead of allowing others to create his mentality for him. This is a veritable fact, and it is one of the purposes of The New Psychology to bring the race to a realization of its truth. Too long has man bowed before what he considered Fate. Man is now learning to be his own Fate.

The fundamental idea of The New Psychology is embodied in the symbol of the charioteer driving his fiery steeds under full control and with taut rein. The chariot represents the being of the man; the charioteer, the Ego; the reins, the will; the steeds, the mental states of Feeling, Emotion, Desire, Imagination, and the rest. Unless the reins be strong, they will not be sufficient to control the horses. Unless the charioteer be trained and vigilant, the horses will run away with the chariot and dash to pieces the driver in the general wreck. But controlled, and mastered, the fiery steeds will leap forward to attainment and accomplishment, and at the same time will travel the road in safety.

And now, as we reach the end of the book, we would remind you that all that you have read will avail you naught if you refrain from acting upon the advice given. If you rest content with the mere intellectual understanding of the subject, you will have gained but little. But, on the other hand, if you will determine to manifest in action the ideas herein taught, you will have started on the road to attainment and positivity.

Each of you is the charioteer driving the fiery steeds with the reins of the will. How are you driving? Are you mastering the steeds, or are they mastering you? It is in your power to curb, control, urge on and direct these splendid mental creatures, so that you may travel far into regions of attainment and accomplishment. Or it is within your power to allow them to wander from side to side of the road, traveling away from the main road, and into the swamps and morasses on the side. Or it is within your power to "give them their heads" and allow them to rush away with you to destruction. Have you decided which of the three courses you shall follow? Have you decided whether you shall be the Master, or the mastered? There comes a time in the life of each one of us when this question must be answered—the course chosen. It may be that this time has come to you, in the reading of this book Are you ready to answer it? Remember the question. It is: "Mastery or Servitude—Which?"

FINIS.